M000078768

THE BENEDICTINES

THE
BENEDICTINES

By

DOM DAVID KNOWLES

MONK OF DOWNSIDE ABBEY

With an Introduction by

J. HUGH DIMAN, O.S.B.

WIPF & STOCK · Eugene, Oregon

Wipf and Stock Publishers
199 W 8th Ave, Suite 3
Eugene, OR 97401

The Benedictines
By Knowles, David
ISBN 13: 978-1-60608-680-3
Publication date 5/14/2009
Previously published by Macmillan, 1930

Nihil Obstat
>Arthur J. Scanlan, S.T.D.
>>*Censor Librorum.*

Imprimatur
>✠ Patrick Cardinal Hayes
>>*Archbishop, New York.*

New York, November 4, 1929.

CONTENTS

INTRODUCTION

The writer of the following pages is already well known to American readers by his admirable little volume on the American Civil War.* In the present book he brings into play the same qualities of analysis, of sympathy and of just discrimination as in the earlier one, but exercises them upon a very different theme.

Benedictines have already had a life of fourteen centuries. This is a long period to compress into a volume of this size, and Dom David Knowles has wisely refrained from attempting a detailed narrative. Instead he has used the past only to throw light on the present and he shows himself more intent upon giving his readers an insight into the contemporary life and spirit of an ancient and almost world-wide religious fellowship than he is upon the external vicissitudes through which it has passed.

Amidst so much that is instructive and illuminating, there is one thought to which the author often recurs and which may perhaps be recommended for special consideration. He says near the close of his book that religious orders are "most valuable not for what they do, but for what they are." This is particularly true of Benedictines, for, unlike most religious orders, they have no prescribed works outside the daily rou-

*The American Civil War, by David Knowles, Oxford University Press, New York.

INTRODUCTION

tine of their monasteries. On the other hand no ex-
terior work, undertaken from the right motives and
under obedience, is denied to them. St. Benedict
himself had no program, either of missionary activity,
nor of charitable action, nor of social reform beyond
the daily round of prayer, of reading and of work
in his own monasteries. What was accomplished by
his followers however outside the monasteries is well
known. In the centuries immediately following St.
Benedict's own day, the face of Europe was almost
literally transformed by his monks. Waste lands
were redeemed, roads were built, the ignorant were
taught, and missionaries carried the faith to the
farthest confines of Europe. Later the ancient classics
were copied and preserved, all the arts were fostered
and pursued, and in the Seventeenth Century the
Maurist Congregation in France brought historical
science and research to their highest point of development.

The torch lit so many centuries ago, but still burn-
ing brightly, was carried across the Atlantic in the
middle of the Nineteenth Century by Dom Boniface
Wimmer and his companions, and to-day stately abbeys, among the greatest in the world, may be visited
in the wide stretches of our own Western land.

These great achievements were the fruit of Benedictine life, but the seeds were sown in the quiet of
monastic routine. Always and everywhere monastic
works are fruitful only as they spring from the love
of God, deepened and ripened in the silence and
prayer of the cloister. All orders are built upon this
root principle, but it is the privilege of Benedictines

to be able to witness to its truth by fourteen centuries of experience.

This thoughtful presentation of some of the deeper aspects of Benedictine life will without doubt strike a responsive chord in the souls of many American readers. It is to be hoped too that this little treatise will help to make it clear that Benedictines in our own day and in our own land, have their mission no less truly than they had it in Europe in those by-gone times that have been named after them, the Benedictine Centuries.

J. Hugh Diman, O. S. B.

THE BENEDICTINES

I

THE RULE OF SAINT BENEDICT

1. *Introduction.*

ALTHOUGH Christianity is essentially a religion of the spirit, it has always maintained the closest touch with the material world. Though its truths are eternal and unchangeable, they were revealed to the world at a definite moment of time, they have been understood more perfectly in this age than in that, and have influenced in different ways different races and generations of men. Hence it has come about that the Catholic Church, though ever one and the same in spirit, has shown in the course of the centuries an almost infinite variety of aspects and developments. Though her deepest life is always hid with Christ in God, she has presented mankind with a more impressive pageant of external activity than has any civilization or empire. Even the most hostile minds have acknowledged the fascination of such a spectacle to one who looks back over the ages; with Macaulay they are overcome with admiration at the institution which carries the mind to the amphitheatre and the catacombs, and is more powerful at the present day than in the ages of faith.

Somewhat similar is the delight of the imagination when directed to one or another of the great religious Orders of the Church. We think of the Franciscans, and even though we may know little of their history or their ideals, the great body of friars rises up before our mind's eye; the original company in what has become to all the world an enchanted landscape of Umbria; the multitudes who passed through every city of Europe before the Reformation; the missionaries who followed the Spaniards and the Portuguese; the theologians and the saints; a Bonaventure, a Scotus, a Bacon, a John Capistran. We think of the Jesuits, and we feel the impression of that mighty impulse, perhaps the greatest single religious impulse since the preaching of the apostles, which spread over Europe from Manresa. We are reminded of Francis Xavier, of Edmund Campion, of Aloysius, of Francis Borgia, of Suarez, of Bellarmine, of Petavius, of de Lugo, of the evangelization of South America and the Indies, of the colleges, the universities, the courts. We think of the Benedictines, and there comes before us a picture of Catholic Europe, her lands covered with great abbeys.

Nowhere are the past glories of monasticism more impressive than in England, and nowhere in England more than in the western Midlands, where the Stratford Avon flows into the Severn. The view from the summit of Bredon hill is one of the loveliest even in England, but it must stand alone in the wealth of historical memories that it recalls. The town that

gave birth to Shakespeare, the battlefields of Evesham, of Tewkesbury, and of Worcester, the homes
of the first movers of the Gunpowder Plot are all
within sight. But the mind goes back more readily
to the England of the great abbeys. At the foot
of Bredon to the north lie Evesham and Pershore,
only a few miles apart; to the west are Worcester
and Malvern, distant from each other less than a
dozen miles; to the south-west is Tewkesbury, and beyond Tewkesbury, Gloucester; to the south-east
Winchcombe, and two or three miles from Winchcombe the ruins of the Cistercian abbey of Hailes,
where on its day of dedication thirteen altars were
consecrated by thirteen prelates. And beyond this
circle of great houses lie the historic names of England—Glastonbury, Ely, Croyland, Bury St. Edmunds, Canterbury, Westminster—and beyond them
again Bec and Cluny, Montserrat, St. Gall and
Einsiedeln, Monte Oliveto, Monte Vergine, Monte
Cassino.

Many of these, whose very names have a beauty
and associations which rival the names of myth and
romance enshrined by Vergil and Milton, have lain
for centuries in ruins, their walls covered with ivy,
their cloisters turned into byres. But in their place
have come others. Solesmes and Pierre-qui-Vire,
Maredsous and Louvain, Beuron and Maria-Laach,
Sant Anselm's on the Aventine; a growing number
beyond the Atlantic, south and north; in Korea, in
Ceylon, in West Africa, and in Australia. And in
England the lineal descendants of the past are already growing to something of the stature of their

3

ancestors. Downside stands midway between the old abbeys of Bath and Glastonbury; Ampleforth not twenty miles from St. Mary's, York, and nearer still to the great Cistercian houses of Rievaulx and Byland; Douai within a few miles of Reading.

This appeal to the imagination which is made by Benedictine history is very strong, so strong in fact as sometimes to hinder us from gaining a clearer notion of Benedictine ideals. Ever since the days of Dugdale, antiquarians have been busy measuring and excavating the ruins of the monastic houses, and for the last hundred years social historians have been attempting, with increasing success, to give us a picture of the life that was lived within their walls. As a result, modern Englishmen are prone to regard monasticism as a feature of a particular society—that of the middle ages—and to regard all that went before as a preparation, and all that has come since as an attempt to revive the institutions of a period of history whose spirit was utterly different from that of to-day. In the pages which follow, scarcely anything will be said of English medieval monasticism. We shall not be concerned with reconstructing the details of life in a Benedictine monastery at any period, or with attempting to understand the outlook of another age. Nor are we concerned with a comparison between the Benedictine form of life and those of other great religious institutes. Our task is to state, so far as possible in a small compass, the positive aims and ideals of that form of life in whatever country and century it has been lived.

THE RULE OF SAINT BENEDICT

2. *The Rule.*

It may be objected at the outset that such a statement of aims and ideals is impossible. Can an institute with fourteen hundred years of existence behind it, born in Italy when the shadow of the ancient civilization still stood, have remained for so many centuries without changes such as to alter its whole essence? We know that even dogmas of the faith have so developed during that period that many details known now by every child were then only implicitly believed by Popes and doctors, and is it possible that a form of life should not have changed? There is a great gulf fixed between our English forefathers of the middle ages and ourselves, how much greater the gulf that separates us from the dark ages!

Again, we know many intimate details of the lives and sayings of Saint Francis and Saint Ignatius Loyola, so that they stand before us quite as clearly as do other historical figures, Innocent III or Charles V; but Saint Benedict is a dim figure, and the facts of his life are given us in a clothing which obscures rather than reveals his personality. Nor have we any documents which throw light on the lives of his early followers.

Such considerations would have weight if Saint Benedict had been, like St. Francis or St. Ignatius, the founder of a religious order who by his force of character and personal attraction set on foot a great movement. But it would seem that the direct personal influence of Saint Benedict upon his contemporaries was very limited. It was not by his activities, or by his personality, or even by his holiness that he influenced so deeply his own and future generations, but by his Rule, and in his Rule we possess a document almost unique in Christian literature, at once impersonal and full of character, which has influenced each succeeding generation of monks in much the same way that the Gospels have influenced religious souls in every age. Only those who have read and re-read the Rule can appreciate the depth which underlies its apparent simplicity, and the greatness of Saint Benedict's achievement in writing what is at once a workable rule of life and a guide to Christian perfection. There are many rules, with a scheme of religious life drawn out in considerable detail, but containing little or no reserve of spiritual teaching. On the other hand there are many spiritual classics, such as the *Ascent of Mount Carmel* or even the *Fioretti* which are so highly individualistic as to give little help to many types of character. Saint Benedict's Rule combines what is best in either group; it is extremely detailed in its directions on all essential and some non-essential points, while, when principles or rules of conduct are in question, every word seems chosen to avoid any suspicion that the writer has in mind abnormal or uncommon types of character. No one seriously aiming at Christian perfection can go to the Rule for help and come away feeling that he has read advice suitable only for a particular call or a particular stage of the religious life. Each finds there what he seeks. The Rule has something of the divine impersonality, without limitations and yet intensely

6

THE RULE OF SAINT BENEDICT

individual, of the Gospel teaching; nor should this surprise us, for the Rule is the Gospel teaching.

But does not the rule of every religious order hold a similar place in that order's history? Not, surely, an exactly similar place. In some orders, such as the comparatively small eremitical and wholly contemplative orders, there has not been, and cannot well be any serious modification or development which is not a clear revolution or relaxation. In the highly organized modern orders, the rule is consulted and interpreted by the governing body in some such way as Scripture is by the teaching body of the Church. But, as we shall see, independence and autonomy, unity in variety and ever-renewed vitality have always been characteristics of Benedictine monasticism. There has never been a fountain-head, a teaching body, to which individual Benedictine houses could appeal. At every rebirth or reform the Rule has been the one inspiring document. As with congregations and houses, so with individual monks. In the life of each monastery the Rule is the one book which every Abbot, every superior, reads and tries to grasp more and more. What wonder then that true Benedictine life and ideals should show little change with the centuries, and that Benedictine abbeys throughout the world, though connected by no legal bond, should be united in spirit?

What then is the Rule? For whom did St. Benedict write, and what was the life he wished his followers to lead?

The Rule is a document a little more than half

as long as the present essay. It is divided into a prologue and seventy-three chapters of very unequal length. Whatever may have been the immediate occasion of its composition,[1] it is written as if for use in a large number of monasteries with locally differing circumstances, and although the daily life and work are entered into in considerable detail, there is scarcely a trace of any legislation dictated by the position of the monastery in which it was composed. Although the Rule is relatively brief, details of the psalms and prayers to be used in the Divine Office, and of the manner and degrees of correction and satisfaction for faults are settled with almost meticulous care; but when the legislator treats of the great monastic virtues and offices, of obedience, of humility, of silence, of the Abbot, of the procurator, every phrase seems to reveal a life's experience and thought. Hence it is possible to extract from the Rule a very fair notion of the time-table and fare of the monks for whom it was written, while on the other hand it remains a source of spiritual instruction unaffected by the lapse of centuries.

Although so short and so methodical, the Rule is not an entirely original work in the sense that many modern and some ancient books are original; that is to say, that in them the outward expression of the thought of the author cannot be traced directly and certainly to an earlier writing. In very many

---

[1] Abbot Chapman has recently brought forward many arguments in support of his view that the Rule was written at the command of Pope Hormisdas for the monks of the Empire.

THE RULE OF SAINT BENEDICT

cases, as a glance at a critical edition of the Rule [1]
will show, the resemblances of general expression and
order between Saint Benedict and earlier Fathers and
monastic writers is far too close to be accidental and
in a considerable number of passages the verbal resemblance is so striking as to prove that Saint Benedict was borrowing phrases and sentences from his
predecessors. The indication of these "sources," as
they are called, is of the highest value and interest as
showing what books Saint Benedict read and valued,
and also as showing his skill in selection and criticism,
but it should not be taken as proving a lack of
originality. Saint Benedict's Rule is original just so
far as is the third scene of Macbeth, or the development of the action in King Lear, or the Sermon on
the Mount; that is to say, it is original in the only
true and deep sense. It is the work of a mind
which has made its own all that was good in the
past, and itself creates something that all future generations will use and enjoy. A textual critic who has
spent months or years in working on a document is
very often the worst judge of its broadest implications
and value. He cannot see the wood for the trees.
Anyone who doubts the originality of the Rule should
read any of the earlier and contemporary rules; he
will then have no doubt as to the impression of a
living, creative personality behind the Rule of Saint
Benedict.

---

[1] The best edition of the Latin text is by Abbot Butler (*Sancti
Benedicti Regula*). There is an English translation by Abbot
Hunter Blair (*The Rule of St. Benedict*).

9

THE BENEDICTINES

Saint Benedict wrote his Rule for all who wished to be monks. To wish to be a monk was, in his own words, "to wish to renounce one's own will." He is legislating, therefore, for those, for all those, who wish to devote themselves to God in a particular form of life. His monastery is a "school of the Lord's service." Everywhere he is positive, constructive. Nowhere does he suggest that he is writing for those who have used the world ill and now repent, for those who have had a past; that the monastic life is a reparation, a *pis aller*. Nor does he suggest that he is writing for those called in some special way to serve God by penance, expiatory sufferings, or intercessory prayer. His invitation is to all, and it is the invitation of the Gospel to the individual soul. He proposes no work, apart from God's service, that he is supplying for the Church; nowhere does he suggest that he is writing for those who wish to work directly for others. He is thinking explicitly only of the salvation of him to whom the invitations of the Rule are addressed. Other works and consequences will come in due time, as necessary means to this end, but Saint Benedict is thinking, as he assumes that his sons will think, not of the means but of the end, and of an end which has its fulfilment not in time, but in eternity.

It is perhaps not out of place, when discussing Saint Benedict's ideals, to remind ourselves that his monks were not priests, and that, therefore, it was none of his business to decide in what relation they should stand to the clerical body. Nowadays, when it has for so long been the custom for all choir religious, even though vowed to the strictest poverty or the deepest seclusion, to become priests, while on the other hand so many orders of regular clerks have been founded, we ordinarily confuse a religious vocation with the call to the priesthood. Moreover, in the course of centuries of good discipline, the ideals of spiritual perfection held up to the secular clergy have come to be hardly distinguishable from those attributed in earlier times to the monastic order, and it is a commonplace that in countries of mixed religion, where the Church is not supported by the State, numbers of the secular clergy have to endure privations as great, if not greater, than those practised in religious houses. But when Saint Benedict wrote all this was different. He had a clear field. The monastic life was a sharply different state from that of the clergy. The life he offered was the only alternative (save the wholly eremitic life or the debased monastic life of the time) to a life in full contact with the world. Since his day this single alternative has been subdivided, and many great religious orders of monks and friars and canons and regular clerks of all kinds aim at essentially the same spiritual ideals as Benedictine monachism. Hence it would be disingenuous to claim much of Saint Benedict's teaching as the peculiar property of Benedictines nowadays. The Gospel counsels are the monopoly of no religious order. It will be therefore necessary, especially in a sketch which is one of a series, to lay some stress on works and ideals which have come to be regarded as peculiarly Benedictine. Nevertheless, we may be allowed to remind

11

ourselves that the Rule, and it may be added, the Constitutions of most Benedictine congregations, aim at nothing more particular than the guidance to God of those who wish to serve Him more fully than is normally possible in the world.

The life which Saint Benedict wished his monks to lead was one in which full scope was to be given to the growth of supernatural motives and supernatural virtues. It was a life to be passed in the presence of God, with every action and activity directed towards Him. It was, therefore, to be a life without distractions, a life of prayer. In this life there were three chief instruments, liturgical prayer, reading and work.

Saint Benedict's legislation on work, and the effect it has had upon the course of European history, have received a full measure of praise from modern historians. The achievement of his monks in this way and in that during the fourteen centuries of their existence has, indeed, been almost incalculable. The reclamation of vast areas to cultivation, the spread of religion and letters in Holland and Germany, the preservation of the manuscripts of the classics, the work of the monastic schools, the labours of the great Maurist scholars in the seventeenth and eighteenth centuries and of some distinguished Benedictine scholars of to-day both at home and abroad—all these works have been generously appraised by many non-Catholic writers and by educated opinion in general, and Catholics (and Benedictines themselves) have been ready enough to accept and echo such tributes. Yet it would be wholly false to Saint Benedict's ideal, and the ideal of the Gospel behind him, to seek to defend monasticism by a recital of its external accomplishments and works. They are indeed a magnificent proof that those who seek first the kingdom of God are able, as it may seem accidentally and by way of *parergon*, but in reality as a necessary consequence of a rightly ordered life, to do work that is both beneficent and permanent for the world. But neither Saint Benedict nor those of his followers who have approached most nearly to his spirit have ever considered their ordinary work as being more than an occupation for that part of their life which remained over from their directly religious duties. Saint Benedict wished his monks to work because he knew that the normal man could not always be either reading or praying vocally, but to attribute to him any purpose of using his institute as a great economic or social or intellectual or even apostolic force would be neither spiritually nor historically true. He wished it to be a great supernatural force and knew well enough that the lesser good result would follow the greater. The work of his rule is an employment—against idleness, as he himself says—for the good of the monk's soul. We may well think also that in Saint Benedict's sane and realist Roman mind there was a conviction that work, man's primeval task on the earth, has a strengthening, bracing, tonic effect on character and soul, and is itself a benediction, almost a sacrament.

Saint Benedict's legislation on reading has not always secured the attention it deserves. Its full implications can only be grasped by those who follow with some care a reconstruction of the daily life in Saint Benedict's monastery and discover that little less than four hours were daily devoted to reading, as compared to some six given to work.[1] Even so we must go a step further, and endeavour to reconstruct the intellectual and spiritual atmosphere of the time. Reading has for the modern world become almost as natural an action as breathing; it is a necessary means to be employed in almost every kind of work that is not merely manual. We have, therefore, come to regard all that we call serious reading as a means to some intellectual end, as the equipment which may help us to act, to speak or to write. It is, in fact, what we call study. With this prepossession, and with the knowledge that all religious institutes of to-day prescribe for their subjects a long and exhaustive course of studies, we are apt to transfer to Saint Benedict's monks the conditions with which we are familiar. This is a serious error. The monks for whom the Rule was written were not students. Their reading was not the means to any practical or intellectual end. Neither knowledge of a practical kind nor learning to be imparted to others by books or teaching was to come of it. It was not even the professional study of divinity made by a clerical body. Saint Benedict's reading was reading done for the benefit of the monk's own soul. It was what we should now call spiritual reading.

---

[1] So Abbot Butler, *Benedictine Monachism*, 2nd edition, p. 287. This is by far the best book on all questions of Benedictine theory, practice and history.

14

THE RULE OF SAINT BENEDICT

Saint Benedict, along with the holy men from whose writings he drew so much inspiration, took a broad, sane view of man's mental as well as his bodily activity. *Nihil volitum nisi praecognitum* was an axiom of the schools long after his day; we cannot love God (and so pray to Him) unless we know Him. How shall they believe Him of Whom they have not heard? We cannot love Him more unless we know Him better; our minds were created to know God as our hearts to love Him; it is not enough that we have at a particular moment of our life put our signature to a creed. Saint Benedict knew that the normal mind, whatever its intellectual abilities, will only be able to advance in prayer and the love of God by an ever-repeated reading of the Bible and those commentaries upon it and the truths of revelation made by the great theologians of the early Church. Meditation, in the broad meaning of the working of the discursive intellect, must precede all prayer that is to be of any value, and will in time come to be wholly pervaded by prayer. Saint Benedict's reading was to be, for each in his degree, at once a spiritual education, a safeguard of the faith, and a prayer. In a well ordered monastery when it was still possible to keep the Rule literally in the circumstances for which it was written, every monk of good will living in such retirement must soon have attained to a consciousness of the presence of God so vivid that his reading would be no interruption, rather a help to keep his heart and mind fixed on Him. Thus there was no need, as there has been for many centuries in the distracted lives

15

of almost all religious bodies, to set apart a fixed time for mental prayer, as it is called. For Saint Benedict's monks, the liturgy and devout reading would normally be a continuous prayer. If a monk felt that for a time reading had done its part and was a hindrance, he could, as the Rule puts it, quite naturally and simply enter the oratory and pray.

In the centuries that have passed since the Rule was written, the Cistercians and Trappists have made peculiarly their own Saint Benedict's legislation on work, and the Carthusians and other strictly contemplative orders have seized and crystallized his reading. Among the direct descendants of Saint Benedict reading and work have in a manner coalesced. They still remain and must ever remain real elements in every true Benedictine life, and their primary influence must always be upon the soul of the individual monk, but their secondary influence has passed far beyond the cloister into the civilization and secondary education of Europe.

The third great element in the monastic life of the Rule is the community prayer, the vocal liturgical adoration of God, the Divine Office, the *Opus Dei*. This long ago became in the eyes of all the distinguishing duty of Benedictine monks throughout the world, and has been recognized so explicitly as their peculiar work by the Church that it is hard for us to set aside for a moment the associations and ideals that have grown up round Saint Benedict's primitive idea, and endeavour, with only the Rule before us, to see what Saint Benedict meant the liturgy to be to his monks. As with work and reading, so with the *Opus Dei*, the simplest and most natural interpretation of Saint Benedict's words is probably the best. The *Opus Dei* was nothing more nor less than the monk's daily prayer, vocal because Saint Benedict, as a Christian, assumed that his monks must serve God with their voices, their gestures, and their attitudes of prayer; made in common because, as we shall see, every important action of his monks was to be done in common. The *Opus Dei*, was liturgical in the sense that every public worship of God is liturgical; but Saint Benedict did not directly intend his monasteries to be, or foresee that they would become, centres of liturgical life. He did not order or expect that they should carry out the elaborate and solemn public worship of God which was then being brought to perfection at Rome, at Milan, at Lyons and elsewhere. He does, indeed, say that nothing is to be put before that *Opus Dei*, but this was not for him the announcement of a policy or an ideal, but a simple interpretation for his monks of the divine command that the direct service of God must occupy the first place among the duties of a Christian. The Office was not considered by him as the end or special function for which his monks existed, but as the necessary offering of service without which no monastic community had any hope or right of existence. Such an attitude of mind towards the Office is perhaps not without its value in an age when all the constituent elements of the Christian life have been isolated and developed in isolation—liturgical prayer, mental prayer, spiritual reading, apostolic work, social work, theological study and the rest. It does not take from Saint Benedict's words any of their force. It shifts the emphasis, but only to lay it more rigorously. The Office for the monk is not merely one of his works or activities; still less, to use a current term, is it a Benedictine "stunt"; it is not even a service that the individual can leave to others; it is for him what his daily or regular prayers are to a Christian in the world, the necessary minimum of his direct service of God.

This it must always remain, if the monk is to be faithful to his Rule; but in view of subsequent developments in the Office we are justified in applying Saint Benedict's emphatic command "Let nothing be put before the *Opus Dei*" to all the forms of solemn liturgical worship which tradition has sanctioned as part of the monastic task. But a review of Saint Benedict's ideas would be misleading which did not, here as everywhere, emphasize his love of the simple and inevitable elements of the Christian life, interpreted in the light of the Gospel counsels.

We are not here directly concerned with the purely spiritual counsels of the Rule, for in these, as in matters of faith, all the saints are one. But there remains an essential condition of Benedictine life which marks it off from much of the earlier monasticism and from some subsequent monastic orders that have confessedly based themselves upon the Rule. Life in Saint Benedict's monastery was a common, not an eremitical, life. The monks were to pray, work, eat, and sleep together; the tools used in ordinary work, the clothes worn on any special occasion, were to be taken from a common store and

returned there after use. The vice of private owner-
ship was to be cut out by the roots. But the spirit
informing this common life was not that of a barracks
or a penitentiary. Saint Benedict's common life is,
as an important reference to the Acts of the Apostles [1]
shows, the common life of the early Christians, not
that of convicts or communists. The common stock
is there for all to draw from, under the Abbot's sur-
vey; more is to be given to one, less to another.

Indeed, we cannot too often repeat, in view of the
superficial austerity of the Rule, that Saint Benedict
nowhere suggests that he is legislating for the no-
torious sinner or, indeed, for any uncommon type
or temperament. His monks are ordinary men, and
he will lead them in a way accessible to ordinary
men. Consequently the note of humanity is found
throughout the strictest legislation on community of
goods; the common life is that of a family with
the Abbot as its father, where the elders love the
younger and the younger honour the elders. The
family spirit which is such a notable feature in every
true form of Benedictine life to-day is no development or adaptation of Saint Benedict's Rule. It is
the teaching of the Rule itself.

Such are the main outlines of the life which Saint
Benedict wished his monks to lead, a life of prayer,
of meditative reading, and of work, lived in common under one common father, and softened by a
spirit of humanity which gave to all the daily rela-

---

[1] "Distribution was made to everyone according as he had
need."—Acts iv, 35. Rule C 55.

tions the help of a natural and a supernatural affection. But before passing on to consider how his life was modified in the course of ages, and what form it has assumed in the modern world, it is as well to remind ourselves that the Rule does not preserve for us a picture of monasticism in its golden age. It is the commonest mistake of monastic writers and reformers to appeal to the Rule as giving us an account of the life of Saint Benedict's model community, and even in this essay "Saint Benedict's monks" have been referred to in a way that might suggest that the Rule was a description of the life led in Saint Benedict's day at Monte Cassino. This, of course, is not the case. Even if we do not consider as certain the view which holds that the Rule was written as a code to be broadcast over the Empire, we have only to look at its contents for a few moments to see that it is no description of life as lived. In fact, two aims and methods run *pari passu* throughout the Rule, and it is precisely this double strand that makes it unique among similar documents. It is half an enunciation of ideals and half a disciplinary code. When Saint Benedict is speaking of humility or obedience, he holds up an ideal of conduct which only a few can ever have realized in practice; when he is speaking of correction and excommunication he seems at first sight to presuppose a great deal of insubordination and contumacy in the community. It is for commentators on the Rule to decide how far these two aspects of the Rule can be harmonized, and how much is due to the circumstances in which the Rule was written. The subject has been mentioned here only in order to avoid idealizing any supposed primitive Benedictine monks. If the Rule were to be taken as a picture drawn from the life we should rather imagine for ourselves a community where corporal punishment was in frequent demand, where monks apostatized and returned in considerable numbers, where they secreted personal belongings in their mattresses, and where even the prior and deans might well behave so badly in office as to deserve degradation. As it is, we may avoid exaggerations in either direction, but we are fully justified in thinking that Saint Benedict had experienced himself, and expected others to realize, that in the kind of life he proposed the most varied types of character and temperament and virtue would be found.

II

BENEDICTINE DEVELOPMENTS

1. *Early Developments.*

WE are to consider in this essay what are Benedictine ideals and what is the Benedictine life to-day, but before doing this it is necessary to notice one or two modifications in the Rule which have been brought about not by the spirit of this or that age, or this or that great man, not by either a decline or a reform, but by a universal custom, even perhaps by an ordinance of the Church, so that they may be taken as legitimate and inevitable developments of Saint Benedict's spirit and ideals.

The first of these was the custom, which in time became the discipline, by which all choir monks (that is, all religious who are not lay brothers) proceeded as a matter of course to receive Holy Orders. In Saint Benedict's monastery, as we know both as a matter of history and from what we can deduce from the Rule, there were only a few priests. He expected that some would leave the ranks of the clergy to become monks, and if necessary the abbot could choose a few for ordination in order to meet the essential religious demands of the monastery. But those so ordained were in the minority. When once it became the custom for the majority or all to be ordained several consequences followed. In the first place, as the custom grew, it was natural that only those capable of a certain intellectual and theological formation should be chosen or allowed to proceed to the priesthood; hence the class of rude peasantry and ex-serfs whose presence in the monastery is presumed in the Rule and attested by Saint Gregory the Great in his Dialogues could no longer hope to be on a perfect equality with all their brethren. At the same time, in an epoch when education of any kind, either theological or secular, was the property of a few, it was natural that those who possessed it should be reserved for work which only they could do. These two tendencies very soon split the single, seamless community of the Rule into two not co-ordinated groups of religious—the priests and those training for ordination, a relatively educated body, engaged in more or less intellectual or administrative employments and recruited from among those who either within the monastery or without had received or were capable of receiving a similar training; and the others, who rapidly became what we should now call lay brothers, a body of uneducated men, engaged on house and farm work, following a different, modified religious observance, under the supervision of the choir monks and recruited from the peasant class. This change (if, indeed, it be an utter change, for some have thought that even at Monte Cassino there were servants from the beginning) was perhaps inevitable, and has certainly never been wholly or permanently renounced by any Benedictine reform or

23

subsequent institute of monks or friars, but its results have been sometimes misunderstood.

The essence of the change was not that monks ceased to do hard manual labour in the fields, for this they had perhaps never regularly done, and certainly in some cases continued to do even when priests. The change was rather that they ceased to be a self-contained body, doing for themselves and in rotation all the domestic works and such crafts as are indispensable in a community's daily life. When once this had come about, they were able to devote the time that Saint Benedict allots to work to other duties, and from these other duties have lineally descended most of the forms of activity pursued throughout the centuries and at the present day by Benedictine monks—a more solemn performance of the Divine Office together with later additions to it, first and foremost among which stands the daily sung conventual Mass; studies, historical and theological; teaching of all sorts, and such quasi-intellectual work as illuminating, copying manuscripts and exercising all the arts and crafts of church decoration.

A second consequence was even more far-reaching than the first. When monks were priests, and had given proof of their sanctity or capacity for administration, it was natural for popes and bishops to choose them out to fill important positions and undertake weighty missions. They were sent, like Saint Augustine and his companions, to carry the gospel to the heathen, or, like Saint Gregory the Great and Saint Isidore of Seville, they were elected to high positions in the Church. Not only individual monks were so

24

used, but whole monasteries came to be regarded as a kind of nursery for future bishops and evangelists. Thus the abbey of Lerins supplied bishops to many cities of the Rhone Valley, and the monasteries of the Low Countries sent forth missionaries to the nations on the shores of the North Sea and Baltic.

In most of these particular cases, indeed, the call was in a sense particular and extraordinary, coming from an ecclesiastical authority outside the monastic body; but the point of importance is that not only individuals, but the monastic body as such, were looked upon as material that could be used at need for the general purposes of the Church.

Along with this spiritual and functional development of the monastic ideal a great change was coming about in the social and economic relations of the monasteries to the country at large. Saint Benedict in his youth had gone into the mountains of Subiaco and lived as a hermit. In time he came to give up the eremitic ideal of the cenobitic, and wrote his Rule for those in community. But the language of the Rule still suggests that the monastery was to be apart from the world, physically as well as spiritually, in no way advertising either its presence or its existence. Whether or not Saint Benedict had any explicit intentions or wishes, the very nature of his institute, a self-contained growing family, living and working upon the land, did not admit of concealment, nor had the celebrated monasteries of Gaul before him escaped becoming part of the life of the country. Very soon all the prosperous monasteries of Western Europe became landowning corporations,

25

wealthy even in spite of themselves, both owing to
their land and to the gifts which flowed in to all
great churches as to the only places of security. In
time, when the feudal system was perfected, the
abbeys took their inevitable place in it, with the abbot
standing to the king as did the great landowning
nobles, and himself having manors and knights' lands
in his possession from which he supplied men of war.
A glance at the chronicles of Jocelin of Brakelond,
which gives a picture of the abbey of Bury St.
Edmunds at the beginning of the thirteenth century,
will show how enormously, and yet how naturally, the
position of a monastery had changed since the writing
of the Rule.

2. *The Middle Ages.*

Such were the almost inevitable modifications of
monastic life which tended to rob Benedictines, both
in theory and practice, of some of that simplicity and
seclusion which are suggested to the minds of readers of the Rule as having been Saint Benedict's ideal,
however rarely attained even in his own experience.
They may, with all their consequences, be described
as the growth—part good, part indifferent, part harm-
ful if not restrained—under conditions of time and
space of the seed of theory and ideal sown by the
legislator. The mustard seed had, indeed, become
greater than all the herbs; it had formed a forest
covering the whole of Europe, and the names most
familiar to the world in the history of the Dark
Ages are those of monks and their monasteries, Greg-

ory, Bede, Anselm, Dunstan, Cluny, Bec, Glastonbury. They carried the Gospel, they reclaimed the soil, they built, they taught, they prayed. Their sound went forth into all the earth, and the times in which they lived have come to be called the Benedictine centuries.

It was neither possible nor desirable that such a state of things should continue; indeed, the wonder is that it should have continued so long. For almost six hundred years, over the whole of civilized Europe outside the Balkans, to be a religious, that is, to serve God according to the Gospel counsels, was to be a Benedictine monk. If a man wished to serve God in His Church without being one of the secular clergy (only too often during those centuries ill-educated and undisciplined in the country districts) he entered a Benedictine monastery. In these circumstances Saint Benedict's Rule was made to comprehend every shade of religious temperament and a great variety of religious observance. That it could do so, and still remain, as it did, a strong and peculiar formative influence, is the strongest of all proofs of its breadth and depth; but as European civilization, and along with it the religious life of Europe, became more complex, more organized, and more self-conscious, it became more and more clear that the Rule of Saint Benedict, hitherto alone in the field, was by itself insufficient to meet all the divers religious needs of the world. Based on the Gospel, and in its leading ideas little more than a commentary upon the Gospel, it had almost the Gospel's breath. Adequate enough, like the early formularies of faith, to meet the demands of its time, it had in no way fallen out of date. Rather, it had now become almost as a genus of the religious life which could not exist save in a number of species more defined than it and marked off by specific qualities each from the other. And so it happened that the various species took form, and the Cistercians, the Carthusians, the Olivetans and the Camaldolese (to name but a few) appeared as bodies of monks alongside of the black Benedictines. Some of these new institutes copied much from Benedictine rule and practice, and were clearly species of the genus; others, such as the Carthusians, while professedly aiming at something different from the monasticism they saw around them, did in fact retain something of Saint Benedict's spirit; others again, such as the Cistercians and in a later century the Trappists, professed to be making a return to the literal observance of Saint Benedict's Rule. There was, indeed, a place in the Church for such an interpretation of the gospel counsels as was given by Saint Bernard of Clairvaux and later by the Abbot of La Trappe; but it is abundantly clear to all who know something of the Rule and of religious history that neither the early Cistercians nor the Trappists comprehended all Saint Benedict's spirit and ideals. They were, indeed, trying to clutch the inapprehensible. A literal interpretation of the Rule had ceased to be possible and true, not merely because the use of flesh meat or the disappearance of corporal chastisement had changed the conditions of religious life, but because no interpretation or practice of the Rule could any

28

longer be at once definite enough and comprehensive enough.

We may take an analogy from the history of the stage. The play Hamlet was written for a particular stage and a particular audience, with a number of conventions both of thought and imagination. It may well be that Burbage, under the direct tuition of Shakespeare, interpreted the part of Hamlet in a way that satisfied even the poet's demands and certainly those of his audience. But since the days of Elizabeth the stage and its conventions have changed beyond all recognition, and while the producers of to-day have immeasurably greater resources it may be that our power of dramatic imagination is considerably less. On the other hand, the experience of centuries and the attention of great actors and critics has revealed depths and difficulties and subtleties in the thought and character of Hamlet which were unsuspected by Southampton and his friends. Should we dare to say that any one method of producing Hamlet would satisfy all the implicit requirements of the play, or that any one interpretation of the part, however touched with genius, would satisfy Shakespeare now, if he could revisit the theatre? What would it aid us if a perfect reconstruction were made of the Globe Theatre, and the play performed with all the actions and gestures authorized by the antiquary? The centuries have left their mark too deep upon our minds. We could never be such as were the Elizabethans.

But if the original institute of Saint Benedict was thus delimited and divided, can any monks claim

THE BENEDICTINES

to be the lineal descendants of his monks? A river
that flowed in a single great channel has split into
a dozen branches near the sea. The waters of each
come from the same source, but each has less water
than the single stream above. Yet even here there is
commonly one channel larger than the rest which
alone preserves the name once common to all. A tree
may have many branches, but there is one main
trunk that goes above them all. So, surely, it is
significant that the common opinion and the discipline
of the Church have never hesitated to keep the name
Benedictine for a monasticism that has never made a
sudden or lasting attempt to check its own gradual
development, and, it may be, its own change; and
that, with all that it may have lost, preserves more
faithfully than any of its derivatives or competitors
the breadth and adaptability of its founder's idea.

This point, which may have been laboured over-
much, is not without importance, for to the casual,
and perhaps even to the careful, reader, the life of
a great Benedictine monastery at the present day, and
perhaps ever since the twelfth century, seems to de-
part more from the Rule of its founder than does
a Charter-house or a Dominican priory or a Jesuit
college.

We have now to consider what were those limitations, that narrowing of the original idea, which are
found in Benedictine history after the multiplication
of orders in the early Middle Ages. Perhaps "limitation," a negative concept, is a less satisfactory word
than "specialization." Experience, both historical

and psychological, seems to show that positive concentration on some work or form of life implies a corresponding limitation in other directions; certainly this has been the case in Benedictine history, and an attention to one or two leading precepts of the Rule has caused one or two departments of the work of the Church to be considered peculiarly Benedictine provinces, at times, even, Benedictine preserves.

The earliest in time of these to develop was the solemnization of the choral Office and liturgy. Pledged by their founder to a care for the *Opus Dei,* which was to come before all other cares, they naturally and inevitably interpreted his command as a direction to devote to a more careful performance of this primary duty whatever time could be saved or made elsewhere. At the same time the development of the sacred liturgy throughout the West and of the Mass as its centre, together with processions of the Host; the elaboration of plain chant as an artistic form of immense variety and flexibility; the economy of time over Saint Benedict's horarium when a wealthy community of priests had numerous lay brothers to do all the menial and craft work, and a host of dependents to till the land—all these pointed in the same direction. Already by the beginning of the eleventh century Cluny had made of the choir duties, prolonged by a number of extra offices, practically the whole employment of a monk, and theoretically his *raison d'être*. Ever since that time the solemn, prolonged, and sometimes even pro-

THE BENEDICTINES

tracted performance of the Divine Office and liturgy
has been a note of Benedictine monachism.

Along with the development of the Office, and
caused by the same causes, went the development
of what may be called in the widest sense higher
religious study, that is, intellectual work devoted,
at least indirectly, to the cause of religion, but not
having as its direct end the ordinary instruction of
the faithful or defence of the faith, but rather the
enriching of the mind of the Church as a whole.
Such a phrase, applied to the work of monks in the
Dark Ages, may sound fanciful, even fantastic, but
if we hope to understand monastic work in any age
we can only succeed by realizing that it was the
same spirit in different times which inspired the
eighth century copyist, the thirteenth century illu-
minator and the seventeenth century Maurist, and
that this spirit in each case was rather that of a religious performing a ritual task of which the final
result was unseen, than of an artist or student working at a subject of his own choosing. As elsewhere,
so here; the secondary good result that all the world
sees—the preservation of the Latin classics, the editing
of the Fathers—flowed from the primary result, the
conscientious daily occupation of the monk. Very
soon after Saint Benedict's day, perhaps even during
his lifetime, the great monasteries came to be regarded as centres of religious learning, and throughout the so-called Dark Ages they stand out, even to
hostile eyes, as sources of comparative illumination.
Schools and seminaries, centres of art and architecture, they remained throughout the Middle Ages,

32

but there was always, and still is, a subtle difference, which we shall try to analyse later, between Benedictine influence in these ways and that of any other religious body, so that we can never identify the monks with an intellectual movement as the friars are identified with early scholasticism, and the Jesuits with the reform of Catholic education all over the world. And for this reason, apart from others, a vague phrase, as is the phrase "higher religious study," is perhaps the best to describe the nature of their work.

There is a third characteristic of medieval Benedictine monachism, perhaps more limiting than these two, though it is shared in part with almost all who derive from the Rule, and it may be said to have been at least implicitly foreseen by its founder. A Benedictine monastery which in a long course of years has had any prosperity, spiritual or material, becomes at once an imposing physical presence, rooted upon the land and bound to the Christian life around it by a thousand material and spiritual ties. In this it differs, in a way visible and comprehensible to the most superficial observer, from even the largest house of friars, and from the largest houses of the more modern orders and congregations. These, fully manned and vibrating with life though they be, are not, so to speak, of the soil. The eyes of those within their walls are turned outside upon the life of the Church as a whole, upon a work that their institute is doing at home or abroad—it may be throughout the length and breadth of these islands, it may be all over the world. They

33

house a population which is for the most part a
shifting one. But the Benedictine monastery is of
the soil. If it prospers, its domain, or at least its
buildings, will increase or change; it has an almost
biological growth and decline, sickness and recovery;
it looks to prosper and to grow, not to live as *a rentier*
in the countryside drawing its livelihood from elsewhere.

And by reason of its growth and of its living
family, Benedictine monasteries from the earliest times
have been large owners of property. Corporate poverty, the poverty of the institution as apart from
that of the individual, has never been a distinguishing mark of Benedictines. Indeed, it is hard to see
how a large and flourishing community, which has
to provide employment on the spot for so many
hands, which may expand indefinitely, and which
remains in existence for century after century, can
ever be in a chronic state of want. The very simplicity of life and energy of labour which should
be a monk's have their reward even in material things.
Certainly there are very few monastic bodies at the
present day, apart from exceptional circumstances,
and even including the most strictly contemplative
orders, who are not owners of property on a fairly
large scale.

Hence a natural tendency, as well as the obvious
supernatural reason, has always made the country
rather than the city the first choice for Benedictine
monks; it is only there that the abbey, like a great
oak, can grow untrammelled. And in fact throughout history whenever a great Benedictine house is

34

found in the midst of a populous city and surrounded by it, it is almost always due to some special reason—the growth of the city as at Westminster, the need for a house at the centre of affairs as at Saint Germain des Près, or the necessity for a house at an intellectual centre as at Sant' Anselmo in Rome.

3. *Modern Times.*

Without making any pretence of tracing monastic history, even in outline, we have considered some of the most important developments and modifications of Saint Benedict's idea during the Dark and Middle Ages. We have seen that from a self-supporting community of which the members were all on an equality and for the most part not in Holy Orders, the monastery had become a double community of choir monks, who were also clerics, and lay brothers. The *Opus Dei*, from being merely the common family, prayer, had become a special feature of Benedictine life; it had been increased and was everywhere performed with solemnity; reading and manual work had coalesced when the employment of monks became largely intellectual; and finally the simple and retired monastery of the early days had become an imposing owner of property, the rival of the greatest landed proprietors of feudal Europe. These marks may be said to have been characteristic of all black Benedictines and of some of their derivatives at the close of the Middle Ages, and they have been found in varying measure in all Benedictines ever since that time.

THE BENEDICTINES

At the opening of the sixteenth century the monasteries of Europe, though swollen with great possessions and on the whole listless, were numerous,[1] powerful and immensely wealthy. The cataclysm of the Reformation swept them away from northern Europe, and though in the territories of the Catholic powers no revolution took place, the spiritual forces of the counter Reformation brought about a gradual re-alignment and reform in Italy, France and the dominions of Spain. In almost every country the new birth was an organization of monasteries more closely knit together than before, and in almost every case, also, the new bodies were less wealthy and more austere of life. It is noticeable, besides, that by the middle of the seventeenth century several Benedictine congregations had accepted the position that they, as a not unimportant member of the Church militant—and a Church now, for the first time for a thousand years, fighting a defensive battle—should do some special work in the interests of the Church as a whole. Among such works we are especially familiar with the achievements of the French congregation of Saint Maur and with the educational and apostolic labours of the exiled houses of the revived English congregation.

At the end of the eighteenth century Benedictine monachism, in common with almost all orders and degrees of the Church, from the Papacy downwards, suffered a reverse more severe in its immediate con-

---

[1] Abbot Butler, *Ben. Mon.*, p. 364, gives the number of Benedictine abbeys at this time as 1500.

sequences than had been caused by the Reformation. The rationalism which had sapped the life of the Church in so many countries was followed by the French Revolution, and after the Revolution came the conquering armies of Napoleon. When the treaty of Tilsit was signed there were fewer Benedictine monasteries in Europe than at any period since the days of Saint Gregory the Great.[1] The French monasteries had disappeared at the Revolution, and with them had gone the exiled English congregation— not indeed to extinction, but to twenty years of precarious lurking in English country-houses. The Bavarian monasteries had for the most part gone, and wherever the French arms penetrated the wealth, and in some cases the homes, of the religious were taken from them. Nowhere was there a stirring of new life; only here and there, and notably among the ancient Swiss abbeys, a few venerable monastic houses stood, like oaks shaken and stripped by a tempest which had torn up by the roots all other trees of the forest.

The new birth came more speedily than could ever have been expected. Little more than half a century after the lowest point had been reached, several of the old national congregations had revived into healthy life; a new movement had gone out from the old Cassinese congregation of Italy, and another across the Atlantic from Bavaria to North America; while in France and the Prussian lands the new congregations of Solesmes and Beuron

---

[1] Their number was reduced to about thirty.

came into being. Almost all these, not excluding some houses which had never lost corporate existence, broke with the immediate past and strove to realize anew the Rule of Saint Benedict in the full nineteenth century unhampered by any tradition save that clear to all in the history of the Church.

Thus the variety of Benedictinism, always great by reason of differing nationalities, is now greater than ever, owing to the subtle difference between the old congregations, at once limited and enriched by their connection with the past, and the new congregations, still inspired by the ideas of their modern founders and bound together by stricter ties of control and dependency. Even the most superficial observer could scarcely fail to perceive this difference when visiting, let us say, Solesmes and Beuron of the one group, and the Swiss Einsiedeln, perhaps the most typical example of the other. The spirit of Saint Benedict is catholic enough to comprehend all this variety, and all Benedictines will rejoice that their increase throughout the world, in the New as well as the Old, has been great within the last century and shows no sign of slackening even after a War which has changed so many currents of empire and of thought.

III

BENEDICTINE ORGANIZATION

HITHERTO the Benedictine institute has been considered externally in its birth and growth. We must now look at its organization, as seen in the Rule as it is interpreted to-day by the living body of monks.

The keystone of Saint Benedict's monastery is the Abbot, and the descriptions of his office and duties in the Rule have justly been recognized as masterpieces of spiritual wisdom. The Abbot stands in the place of Christ; the monks are his, that he may lead them to God; he is their shepherd, as Christ is of all men; it is from him that God, the Master of the estate, will demand an account of the souls he has had under his hand; every fault of theirs will at the last judgment be charged to him, and upon him will lie the burden of the proof before he can be absolved from having caused their ruin.

On the other hand, the obedience of the monks must be absolute; they have renounced their own wills; that is why they have come into the monastery; they can rely on their Abbot as upon their divine Lord, and it is their security that the Abbot's will is for them God's will, with no possibility of doubt, which gives to their obedience its value and its joy.

THE BENEDICTINES

Needless to say, Saint Benedict's teaching on obedience is as practical and as valuable to-day as it ever was, and the monk's obedience as absolute. It gives to Benedictine life, as it gives to all religious life, a firmness and a sanctity which is the source of all its strength. At the same time, there have always been, and are still, some characteristics of abbatial government which are not found in every religious organization. In the first place, the very name "Abbot," "Father," suggests a relationship, suggests that the Abbot cannot exist apart from, or act without a thought for, his monks. He is not merely one in a hierarchy of rulers; he is Abbot only of, and because of, his monks; his power of command and their vow of obedience are complementary and coincident, and both exist only for the good of the monks' souls, not for the more efficient working towards any other end, however good. The Abbot is not a colonel who acts under the orders of a brigadier, nor a Speaker who acts as intermediary between the monastery and the world, nor a monarch who has for the time being so much material with which to work. The Abbot may not exploit his monks. He may not even regard them as so much man-power to dispose of for the good of the Church.

Moreover (though this applies in a measure to every religious superior), the Abbot is in a real sense the servant of his monks. He is to lead them to God, not in his way or at his pace, but in the way God wishes for each. He must, in Saint Benedict's own words, realize what a hard task is his, to wait upon the different characters of his monks, and nothing in the Rule is more striking than Saint Benedict's insistence that the sheep may be killed by over-driving, the vessel broken if scoured too fiercely. *Ne quid nimis*, be not over zealous, he says to the Abbot; and he warns him that the standard he sets should be below that which the strongest of his monks will desire.

The Rule, whatever its immediate destination, was written for a number of monasteries bound together by no confederation and with no regular place in the life of the Church. Before Saint Benedict's day not all these had a written Rule, but each had an Abbot. It is natural, therefore, to find that direct commands from the abbot are assumed in the Rule as necessary for every detail of the daily life. Possibly, too, Saint Benedict transferred to the Abbot of his Rule some of his own experience. In all religious origins and reforms the *ipse dixit* of a saint of tried wisdom and experience is everything to his followers, for he has all the qualities natural and supernatural that win a ready rational obedience and satisfy our craving for sight rather than faith. Certainly the impression gained from reading the Rule is that the Abbot was to be an influence actually, and not virtually, operating upon the lives of his monks throughout the ordinary day's routine.

But we need not think that a monastery has fallen from Saint Benedict's ideal if the monks are not perpetually receiving commands and directions from the Abbot. The growth of canon law, with all the obligations it imposes on clerics and religious, the development of a tradition in the spiritual and monas-

41

tic life, the age-old *mos majorum* which even the
Rule encourages, all these often take the place for
Benedictines of the direct commands of the Abbot.
Nor is it necessary to emphasize that in a highly
educated civilization, where books can in a moment
supply the traditional answer to so many difficulties,
and where organization demands uniformity, far more
must be left to the discretion and to the conscience
of the individual monk than was desirable or possible in the mixed communities, to whom the Rule
would come as a new and strange thing. We may at
times regret the simplicity of an earlier age, when
the direct command stood where now is an anxious
weighing of motives, but it is as useless to wish that
simplicity back as it would be to wish for the loyalty
of a feudal baron in the political life of to-day, or for
a grown man to wish for the uncritical docility of
his childhood. The spirit may always be the same;
the principle of obedience still stands; the implicit
will of the Abbot is expressed in the rules and customs of the house, and from time to time there
will come a sufficiently searching test of direct obedience.

In spite of Saint Benedict's clear teaching of the
personal responsibility of the Abbot for the spiritual
well-being of the individual monk, there is perhaps
no essential point of the Rule that has been so often
neglected in practice. When once the abbeys of
Europe became landed corporations with a recognized
place in the civil order, and especially under the
feudal system, it was essential that they should be
represented before the world by one of their number

42

capable of defending their rights. Naturally this duty fell to the Abbot, and as a result the great medieval Abbot was a personage apart from the community, with an establishment, domains and a career of his own. During a large part of the year he used as his residence one or other of his country houses or his town house, rather than his monastery, and even in the monastery he had separate quarters from the monks.

corrupt abbot

This condition of things, though scarcely ideal, was at least virile, but worse was to come when, throughout Europe, the system of *in commendam* was extended to the greater abbeys, and the abbacy and its revenues were held by a non-resident dignitary of the Church, or even by a layman and a child.[1] A way of government bad in theory may do well enough in practice, and in very many cases the claustral prior filled the position of Saint Benedict's Abbot with temporal and spiritual success; but the system as such was intolerable, and this was one of the abuses most attacked and guarded against by the Benedictine reforms of the counter-Reformation. At the present time throughout the world the relations between Abbot and monks are probably more nearly those intended by Saint Benedict than at any time since the days of Charlemagne. The danger, however, remains, if not in large affairs then in small, that the Abbot, in his capacity of administrator, landlord and prelate, may forget that the welfare,

corrupt monastery

[1] This system was never extended to England except by Wolsey.

43

Abbot is busy and sometimes forgets monks' spiritual health

spiritual and temporal, of the individual monk is within his responsibility, and that the care of it, in the last resort, cannot be delegated to any subordinate official. It is the government of souls [1] that he has undertaken; all else is in order to this.

All who have written on the Rule in recent years have laid stress on the wide, in fact supreme, powers given by Saint Benedict to the Abbot. Perhaps the tendencies in the nineteenth century towards democracy and committee government, the growth of parliaments and boards, and still more recently of trades unions, workers' councils and soviets, have led Benedictine writers to insist that whatever may be the fashion in the political world of the day, a monastery is ruled by one superior and its chapters are not board meetings. If now, as seems not unlikely, there is a movement of thought in the opposite direction, and an age of direct control is succeeding to the parliamentary epoch, it may be worth while to point out that Saint Benedict, in all matters that are not purely spiritual, points the way, not, indeed, towards a religious democracy, but towards a degree of co-operation between Abbot and monks that can have found few analogies in the decaying civic and political life of his time. The third chapter of the Rule, which follows immediately after the chapter defining the office of Abbot, deals directly with the calling in of the monks to give counsel to the Abbot. This has to be done wherever anything of moment is to be decided; and it is clear from the words of

---

[1] This is repeated four times in the Rule.

44

what is a prior? Abbot?

BENEDICTINE ORGANIZATION

the Rule that the Abbot is to come for help and for
to be done. He is not merely or primarily asking
advice in order that he may then decide what is
his monks for permission to act in a certain way.
When lesser matters are in question the seniors only
are to be consulted; but when it is a question of ap-
pointing a prior (for whom the monks themselves
may ask) counsel must be taken, and the monks are
themselves to choose [1] their Abbot—a command that
shows no small faith in human nature when we
consider the period of history at which it was given.

on big matters monks vote

No change has been made in most Benedictine
congregations in the method of electing the Abbot
and in his internal government of the monastery, but
experience and the growth of canon law have set
certain limits to what an Abbot may do in external
administration without the support of the majority
of his community. Necessary and inevitable as such
legislation is, it is in some ways a decline from the
Rule. Not only may it suggest that in all important
financial and administrative matters the community
is a voting body, over against the Abbot; but it may
reduce the co-operation of Abbot and monks by making the gathering of a chapter seem necessary merely
to give legal authority to an act of government. In
this matter, as in so much besides, Saint Benedict's
statesmanlike wisdom and trust in human nature is
apparent under the seeming simplicity of the Rule.
Few, even among gifted and holy men, are capable

---

[1] "Choose" not "elect" because the actual appointment of the
Abbot came from an outside authority.

45

of combining initiative and receptivity in the ideal proportions; and most legislators in things temporal and spiritual have spent time in devising checks and obligations to safeguard rulers from interference and subjects from the consequences of human weakness. Saint Benedict prefers to legislate in broad lines which point to the ideal and leave it possible for the ideal to be realized, while he warns against the failings that may occur in practice.

The Rule knows of no confederation of monks beyond the individual abbey. The Rule itself, "the holy Rule,"[1] not the legislator or his own community, was to be the only form of monastic life. Here, too, Benedictines throughout the centuries have made no essential change, and remain at the present day unique among the greater institutes of regulars in the Church. There is no Benedictine "Order" in the sense that the Dominicans and Jesuits are an order, with provinces, provincials and general.[2] The individual abbeys are autonomous. All have a spirit and traditions, and often works and religious practices, to a greater or less degree their own, not shared by other monasteries of the same nationality or in the same congregation. In most cases (and this is so in the English congregation) a monk cannot be transferred by his superiors from one autonomous house to another; still less is there any legal connec-

---

[1] So named by St. Benedict in Chapters 23 and 65.

[2] The Latin word *ordo* in the phrase *religiosus ordo* may mean either "ordered way of life" or "organized body." In English the word order has been restricted to the second meaning, whereas only the first applies to Benedictines.

tion or passing of monks between the different
congregations of the world. The Rule and monastic
tradition, open to all in the monuments of the past,
are the only common influences. For the purpose
of maintaining religious discipline, groups of monasteries have from time to time been formed with
common statutes and an Abbot-President or Abbot-
General who has certain powers of visitation and
definition. These congregations, as they are called,
are sometimes national, sometimes international, as
the result of a particular movement or reform. In
some cases the bond between the houses composing
them is strict; in other cases, as in the English congregation, very light, but in no case is there any legal
connection between congregations, and there is no
superior with jurisdiction over all the monks of the
world. Yet perhaps no more impressive proof that
modern Benedictine monasticism is a true development of the original can be found than the undoubted
similarity of ideals and spirit that unites all Benedictines throughout the world. At the international
theological college of Sant' Anselmo in Rome young
monks from all over the world meet and form an
always changing community. A monastic family
in the full sense it can never be, for the individual
members look with true Benedictine affection to the
family of their profession, but the family likeness
among all is unmistakable. If it may be permitted
to give what is only a personal impression, I would
say that at Sant' Anselmo there existed a far greater
similarity of outlook—a common *weltanschauung*—
in religious things between the different nationalities

(and this when I saw it, was only three years after
the Treaty of Versailles, and when many of the
monks had fought and suffered on opposite sides)
than would have existed between any of the nationalities and their fellow-countrymen at the other Roman
colleges. To one unfamiliar with Benedictine institutions this may not seem unusual; but to one
brought up in the isolation of a single Benedictine
abbey it was a welcome and impressive experience.

Truly Benedictine also was the freedom left to
each one in his religious life.' There were gathered
together a hundred young monks, many of them sent
across the ocean away from their monasteries for half-
a-dozen years of the utmost importance in their religious formation. It was a great responsibility for
those under whose care they came. Yet, beyond the
Office and a daily set period for mental prayer before
the Blessed Sacrament, there was no religious exercise, private or common, prescribed. During the
course of the year no additional devotions were im-
posed beyond the customary Benedictions on Sun-
days and feast days. Everyone was left in complete
freedom to choose what spiritual books he wished
and visit the church for further prayer, or not, at
will.

IV

BENEDICTINE WORK

AND so we have arrived at what is in truth the chief end of this study, a consideration of Benedictine monachism as it exists in the Church to-day, one mansion among many. What do Benedictine monks give as their share to the whole of Christian work and praise? Or—to go a little deeper—what is there peculiar in their interpretation of the Gospel counsels?

Before attempting to answer the easier of these questions—What is the peculiar work of Benedictines?—it is worth while to repeat that, strictly speaking, there is no peculiar Benedictine work; no one employment or kind of employment, speculative or practical, intellectual or physical, to which one who enters a Benedictine monastery may expect to find himself destined. This monastery or that, this or that congregation, may be largely or even principally (though this is rare) devoted to a particular form of work—education, research, missionary activity—but there is no single external activity common to all the Benedictine congregations of the world; and in what may be called the most normal Benedictine congregation neither the congregation as a whole nor each house taken by itself has any one outstanding work, suitablity for which is demanded

*Just be a Benedictine

49

*Primary goal /
acheived by diff.
means!*

from all candidates as a condition *sine qua non*
before profession. Here, indeed, is the Benedictine's
heritage from his Founder. He does not exist to
do this work or that, but to serve God and save
his soul. Benedictines are, as we have seen, not
an Order, but a way of life, and not an extraordinary way, but an ordinary way, if any way based
on the Gospel counsels can be called ordinary.

Yet in the Rule, if anywhere, the necessity for
work is insisted upon, and the great variety of activities in which Benedictines have taken part is in
many ways due to their freedom from limitation.
As Christians they refuse no work that is religious
in its scope. Such work may be of very great variety,
but it is normally such as can be accomplished within
the framework of community life, with attendance at
the common prayer. As a result of these conditions,
normal Benedictine work has the characteristic that
it is in most cases consciously felt to be a corporate
work. The force which results from the work is
not merely a thrust which is the sum of all the individual thrusts of those who are co-operating—
that is the case with all team or united work; it is
rather a thrust different in character from anything
that individuals contribute, and which owes all it
has to the past and present life of the house. We
think of Saint Augustine and his monks coming
from Rome to preach the Gospel to England, not
as individuals, as we might imagine the early Jesuit
missionaries, but as a group; still more do we think
of the group rather than the individual in such a
typically Benedictine work as the Maurist scholar-

ship. An example of such a work to-day is the
critical and constructive presentation of plain chant
by the monks of Solesmes Abbey. However this
may have been directed or inspired by one or two
musical scholars of exceptional ability, it is not so
much their efforts as those of a large band of name-
less workers; not so much these, again, as the whole
force of a great abbey in money and books and
ability to test choral music practically; and not so
much this as the age-old Benedictine tradition which
makes everything to do with the Office the monk's
primary duty, and is a guarantee to the authorities
of the Church that a liturgical movement could not
be shaped by better hands.

Similarly, a successful Benedictine schoolmaster or
headmaster is not, as in other schools, a stranger
who has been formed in this school and that university, and has then made his mark and acquired
his experience at half-a-dozen large schools till he
is chosen, because he is what he is, to be headmaster
of Winchester or Harrow. He is rather a represen-
tative to the world for the time being of that community, ever changing, but never wholly changed,
which is the cause of the school's existing and which
gives to all its activities a support and a guarantee,
a setting far more dignified and a goodwill far more
extensive than could be given by a staff of more
brilliant attainments.

And even when a scholar seems to the outside
world to stand alone, a Gasquet or a Cabrol or a
Morin, with a name familiar to all, it will usually
be found that behind him and around him is the

support, not only of a number of his brethren, but of the resources, the traditions and the experience of a great religious house.

The monks, then, of any large monastery, taken as a group, will represent a wide diversity of interests and training. Although in almost all the countries of the world to-day they will have received a good secondary education and in many cases a university education also, and although they will have passed through the normal course of ecclesiastical studies prescribed for the whole Church by canon law, they will not necessarily have all passed through a single intensive theological formation such as is associated (at least by those outside) with the Dominicans and the Jesuits. Needless to say, they will not be, as a body, learned, nor a community of students, but it will be natural to expect that out of a large community which had been long established in a settled country and has as one of its possessions a good library, there will be one or two or more engaged upon some solid work of learning. When this is the case, monastic tradition and the circumstances of the life seem to suggest that there is a normal field of Benedictine studies beyond which they will not generally travel. This does not lie in the realms of abstract or applied mathematics nor in such sciences as biology or anthropology, nor even in philology and literature, but rather in history in all its branches, including positive theology and the critical reconstruction of ancient documents.

But besides this there must always be some work or works which can employ the bulk of the com-

52

munity, at once sufficiently permanent and general
to suit a variety of temperaments and capable of being added to or reduced from time to time as need
arises. Benedictine history and modern practice show
two or three works peculiarly suitable. There is, first,
the care of souls. This, like all Benedictine work,
should be distinctively monastic, that is, it should
normally be done by a monk resident in his monastery
and should be felt to be the work of one of the
community rather than of an individual priest. It
may take the form of ministering to the spiritual
needs of those immediately round the monastery,
whether in country or town, or of systematically giving retreats or instructions to those who are attracted
to the abbey as a centre of liturgical and spiritual
life. Examples of such work can be found in almost
every congregation. The monasteries in England,
apart from the parishes they serve, in almost every
case have round them a circle of small country
chapels; the best example of a large town parish
is perhaps that served by the monks of the Abbey
of Saint Boniface in Munich. The abbeys of
Beuron and Maria Laach in Germany occupy at the
present moment a quite peculiar place in the Catholic
life of the country as centres where non-Catholics of
taste and education become acquainted with Catholic
liturgy and doctrine. Striking examples of what
was in the Benedictine centuries the Benedictine work
par excellence—the evangelization of the heathen and
backward peoples—are to be found in the work of
the Spanish monks in north Australia, of the

THE BENEDICTINES

Silvestrines in Ceylon and of the Bavarians of Saint Ottilian in Korea and East Africa.

Abroad on the continent of Europe many Benedictine monasteries have been founded at, or have themselves become in the course of ages, shrines of pilgrimage, and one of the principal works of the monks is to minister to the needs, corporal and spiritual, of a constant stream of pilgrims. Among such Benedictine shrines are Einsiedeln in Switzerland, Montserrat in Spain and Monte Vergine in Italy. The religious value and suitability of this work for monks is too clear to need emphasis. Whatever may have been the case in the past, devotion to the Blessed Sacrament, shown in the reception of the sacraments of Penance and the Holy Eucharist, is a feature of all modern pilgrimages, even of the vast and popular Neapolitan pilgrimages to the holy picture of Monte Vergine, and the preparation of the pilgrims for this is a truly apostolic work.

Lastly, there is the work of Christian education, which has been an accepted monastic employment as far back as records go, and which can appeal for sanction to the Rule itself and the accounts of the life of Saint Benedict. This may take the usual form of a great school, including in its departments what in England is called a preparatory school as well as the main public school, and thus receiving boys from ten to eighteen years of age; or, (as in the case of some American abbeys) the monks may supply the staff of a diocesan seminary, or even (as at Salzburg) the faculties of a Catholic university.

Work such as this has obvious practical and

54

spiritual advantages. It is a work for religion, carried on within the monastic enclosure; it is essentially a community work which gives scope for many differing characters and abilities, and in which the *genius loci* can have the greatest influence; it brings in a means of support which bears some relation to the labour expended, and which therefore is a certain safeguard against the idleness which in the past has been the ruin of richly endowed foundations—a danger foreseen by Saint Benedict himself; it is a source, direct and indirect, from which the community may hope to gain new members. On the other hand, and especially at the present day and in English-speaking countries, it is a taxing and absorbing work which implies much contact, not strictly religious, with the world, and which tends more and more to assimilate itself, at least in externals, to non-Catholic educational work; also, the recurrence of considerable periods of vacation creates an ebb and flow of work which is not wholly desirable. However, these difficulties are to a large extent accidental, and the work itself is so necessary and suitable that it will in all probability continue to be one of the chief employments of monks for all time.

Finally, there are many kinds of work, half sciences, half crafts, which the monastery may do. This may take the form of some liturgical study and publication, such as the execution, teaching and publishing of Gregorian music by the monks of Solesmes; or it may be a school of art with all its processes of reproduction and execution, as at Beuron; or it may be even the secular Benedictine work of farming and the

selling of some specialized product, as at the Devon-
shire abbey of Buckfast.

This list of Benedictine works may seem to comprehend almost every kind of possibility for religious,
but certain features—that the work is stationary and
in some sense corporate—are common to all those
mentioned above. And beyond this, freedom, the
wide freedom of Christianity, is Saint Benedict's own
legacy to his children, and the constitutions of the
English congregation are fully in the spirit of tradition when, after mentioning three special works—
apostolic, educational and learned—they add, "but
no labour, whether intellectual or manual, which is
religious in its scope and is in accord with the principles of the monastic institute, can be unsuitable to
a monk."

And from this refusal to be pledged to any single
type of activity, from this reserve of life, comes a
Benedictine characteristic which can have escaped
the notice of few, and which yet is difficult to analyse.
It is seen in all external Benedictine activity. In the
realm of dogmatic and mystical theology it is an independence, a freedom from historical connexions and
controversies. Dominicans, Franciscans, Jesuits,
Carmelites, Augustinians—all these are found throughout the ages ranged on this side or on that in the
great controversies which have shaken the schools.
They have a prejudice, an *esprit de corps*. Benedictine
theologians (and there have been many) have always chosen for themselves. They are unconsciously
faithful to their founder's idea; they represent
the ordinary developed Christian, the man in the

street, at once beneath and above schools of thought.

And as certainly there is a disposition among non-Catholics of education and intelligence to regard the literary work of Benedictine monks (often indeed without reason) as more positive, more objective, less tendencious, than equally meritorious work done elsewhere. This no doubt is partly due to the legend of the Maurists, whose patient and selfless work has been popularized by a succession of anti-religious writers from the time of Gibbon; but the cause probably lies deeper still.

Equally, it is not to a group of Benedictine monks, but to some of the secular clergy or friars or members of the Society of Jesus that the average Catholic looks for a lead, and whom he expects to find at the most actual, living heart of the intellectual life of the day, creating and advancing upon the best religious public opinion. The monks were not among the leaders of scholasticism, or of the counter-Reformation, or of the Catholic revival of the nineteenth century. There is something very typical in the appearance of Benedictine monks in the lives of those great religious thunderbolts, Saint Francis of Assisi and Saint Ignatius of Loyola, not in the rôle of disciples or evangelists of the new movements, but as old corporations ready to give a countenance and a modicum of help to whomsoever should come to them consumed with a new zeal.

We said, when beginning this enumeration of Benedictine external work, that it must normally be such as can be accomplished within the framework of community life. Can Benedictine monks ever safely abandon this prinicple? Clearly, they can never abandon it as a thing of no importance; they can never abandon it of their own choice. The passage in the Rule directed against the Gyrovagi or Wandering monks is well known, and though the Gyrovagi were peculiar to the age of Saint Benedict, there is no doubt but that he would have disapproved with equal energy of the wandering monks who are found throughout the centuries, and who entered English literature in the person of Chaucer's fellow-pilgrim, Dom Piers. He, it will be remembered, took little heed of the proverb that a monk out of the cloister is as a fish out of water; but the antiquity of the saying, which has been traced back from century to century to Sozomen and even to Saint Anthony, is a sufficient proof of its truth; and anyone who knows anything of monasticism will appreciate the dramatic fitness of such contempt expressed by one who combines in his person most of the petty monastic foibles and laxities of all the ages.

But, it may be asked, if residence in a monastery is so essential, how is it that considerable numbers of Benedictine monks in various countries of the world live outside their monasteries in a manner indistinguishable from the secular clergy or other religious?

The answer may be given that in all those countries exceptional circumstances, in the past or present, have caused the highest authorities of the Church to call upon such priests as existed anywhere to aid in spreading or maintaining religion in certain districts—

BENEDICTINE WORK

England in the Penal Days, America yesterday and to-
day—and that when such a need has once been felt
and such a call made, a complicated system, ecclesiastical and financial, comes into being which cannot readily be altered, and which, in view of the innate disposition of the Church to let well alone, *quieta non
movere*, will probably never be directly altered from
above. When such a system exists, the monk who
accommodates himself to it is no Gyrovagus; he is
obeying, explicitly or implicitly, the Supreme Pontiff,
the *abbas abbatum*. The Gospel must always be
preached, whereas no religious institute can at any
given time be said to be essential to the Church. In the
cases just mentioned the authorities of the Church have
said, in effect, that parish priests or missionaries are
so sorely needed that monks must take their places.
Saint Benedict, as we have seen, founded his form
of monastic life, not to fill any place in the external
life of the Church, but to create a school of the
service of God, a place where the full Christian life
of the counsels might be lived, a life suiting those
who, with the young man of the gospel, wished to
be perfect. There is nothing in such a life and training to render a man unfit for any other kind of life
whose direct end is the service of God and man.
Nor, on the other hand, does there seem any reason
why a man who has attained to a certain degree of
maturity in the monastic life should be at all harmed
spiritually by a life directed to God's service outside
the enclosure of his monastery. Neither habit nor
choir nor community life are essential to sanctity
and a life of prayer; if the end of all monastic ob-

59

servance, the monasticism of the soul, be once attained, it may be retained *ubique terrarum*. The monk and the contemplative, like Plato's guardians, may come back to the world they have left and be able to work in it and for it. From the earliest times popes and kings have summoned monks, even of the strictest and most retired life, to rule churches.

But while Benedictine tradition has always admitted such changes of life for the tried and the perfect, or in special circumstances, it has not regarded them as belonging to the normal course or development of Benedictine life. It is for the Church to call in the aid of monks to a particular work, and for monks to meet such a call of necessity with ready obedience, while they remember that the Church herself has always maintained a distinction between the pastoral and the monastic vocations, and regarded the sending of monks to pastoral duty outside the common life as something exceptional. A monk who under the call of obedience is summoned to undertake such labour will, without losing any of his monastic character, be able to do a great work for the Church. It may even be said that he will do that work, whatever it may be, with especial success precisely because of his monastic training, for an experience of the full religious observance gives a kind of character and groundwork for life. Yet if we were to argue that a life, lived thus outside the cloister, is a normal Benedictine one, or is the exact equivalent of the life presupposed by the Rule, we might justly be accused of paradox.

A great Benedictine bishop of our own time has

given in a few words what has been the constant Benedictine tradition. "Whatever the external work to which a monk may find himself called," writes Bishop Hedley, in the course of an explanation of Benedictine stability, "the normal thing must always be, to live in his own monastery. It would be a mistake to encourage anyone to profess himself a Benedictine unless he could look forward with pleasure to live, 'for better, for worse,' till death itself, in the house of his profession, under the Rule, and in the daily work of the choir." In the fourth chapter of his Rule, Saint Benedict gives a long list of the instruments of good works, "the tools of the craft of spirituality," as he calls them, which his monks are to use. Among them, it is interesting to note, are many corporal and spiritual works of mercy. At the end he speaks of the workshop where these tools are to be used. It is "the monastic enclosure and stability in the monastic family." And at the end of the Prologue which is a small Rule in itself, he says that his monks will persevere in their monastery even till death. For him it was not a principle, but an axiom, that a monk, as such, lived and worked and died in his monastery.

main thing is stability

V

SOME BENEDICTINE CHARACTERISTICS

CARDINAL NEWMAN, in a celebrated passage,[1] has spoken of the monk's life as poetical, and as affording matter for true poetry. Newman was far too deep a thinker to mean by this that a monk's life should be something romantic, ethereal, unreal, imaginative, an escape from the realities of life. By the poetry of the monastic life, as is clear from what he writes elsewhere, he wished to suggest that a life like those of the early monk-missionaries, a life spent in simple and elemental surroundings and in close contact with the earth—garden, wood and field—as well as with the spiritual world, precisely because it was not self-conscious, had a solemnity and a beauty denied to a more frothy, noisy, artificial existence, and therefore was as fit a theme for poetry as are all the elementary works and emotions of mankind. The monastic life was in fact the stuff of which poetry is born, objective, material poetry.

Yet Newman's phrase was perhaps a little unfortunate, for there is no doubt that Englishmen, both Catholic and non-Catholic, have had, at least since

---

[1] In his essay *Mission of the Benedictine Order.*

the beginning of the Romantic movement, a romantic conception of monasticism. That is to say, the
words monk and monastery have (however subcon-
sciously) borne in their minds something of the same
relation to the actual monks and monasteries of the
Middle Ages or contemporary Europe that the knights
of Keats and Tennyson bore to the contemporaries
of Sir Walter Manny. The greatest of the romantics,
Sir Walter Scott, was merely the most influential of
a long series of novelists and poets who pictured a
race of men at once inhuman and superhuman,
ethereal and fanatical, remote from modernity and
yet subtly attractive, as inhabiting what are now
the ivy-clad ruins and defaced cloisters of the great
monastic houses. They made no serious attempt
to rationalize such imaginations, or to transfer to
the Middle Ages the common human feelings and
failings. Still less did they draw any distinction between the strictest and most contemplative bodies of
religious and those who, though not lax, were less
austere. They could imagine an angelic monk and a
diabolical monk, but they never seriously attempted to
imagine an ordinary human monk. We are still in
spite of ourselves heirs of this tradition, and the
monastic habit, unlike the clerical costume, and even
unlike the nun's veil, still has its romance, its escape-
value, and brings with it a suggestion of the discipline
of fasting and of the midnight office. And this undoubtedly influences the common judgment as to what
the life and practices of monks should be. If we
wish to see true we must be content to go *terre-à-
terre*, to be realists, not romanticists. The last survivor

of the ancient Abbey of Westminster, the last medieval monk, Dom Sigebert Buckley, was a connecting
link between the old and the new English congregations. We are told that Father Augustine Baker,
one of the first monks of the revived congregation
and himself an antiquary, "mightily sought from the
venerable old man" the way of living in the old
monasteries. Unfortunately, he could tell them little.
He remembered, he said, that at Westminster they
rose at midnight, and at supper had first a dish of
cold sliced powdered beef, and next after a shoulder
of mutton roasted.[1]

And there is another danger in approaching a
consideration of the monastic life, more subtle and
more pervasive. It is a manner of thought which
in its most familiar form had its origin in the controversies that followed the Reformation. It is a
kind of Puritanism or Jansenism, a separating of
actions into the religious and not religious, sacred
and profane, worldly and supernatural—a Manicheism
which is alien to the simpler conceptions of the
Gospel. We have all fallen into the habit of not
regarding our life as a whole, but of dividing it
into the religious and the worldly, and though we
know well enough that only a percentage of our
actions can belong to the former class, yet we feel
that whenever we are not employed in directly religious work our right hand should not know what
the left is doing. As a result, some religious think-

---

[1] Weldon, *Chronological Notes of the English Benedictine
Congregation*, Ch. 18.

ers, especially those who are unsympathetic to the
Catholic Church, are inclined to expect of monasticism more than it has ever given or claimed to
give. They expect a monk—and indeed a religious
of any kind—to be occupied directly and permanently
with God, to be at all times and places visibly apart
from the world—the world forgetting, by the world
forgot. Such critics when they are not Catholics
are almost always those who fail to appreciate or
understand the life of the counsels, or of any divi-
sion between more perfect and less perfect in the
Christian life. They imagine that pure monasticism
is only found where there is a complete separation
from the world; they both disapprove of this as
an ideal and find fault with all those who have failed
to realize it fully in practice. They misrepre-
sent because they misunderstand, and misunderstand
still more the creature of their misrepresentation.

Akin, and still deeper perhaps, because more personal, is the desire among religious thinkers for
simplification and renunciation—not of self, for that
can never be too thorough, but of material satisfac-
tions and intellectual occupations. We long for a
Monism of the spirit. Undoubtedly some souls are
thus led to God; but there is a danger lest the un-
compromising logic of such renunciation, and the
intellectual intolerance and limitations of even the
holiest, may canonize such a life, not only as a very
high religious state, but as the only high religious
state. It is a last infirmity of noble minds. Twice
at least in monastic history has a gifted and holy
religious reformer proclaimed such a doctrine. Twice

has it fallen to a Benedictine monk to defend what seemed the less noble cause, but in each case the moral victory has been his. No better expositions of Benedictine ideals and aims have ever been framed than the defences of Peter the Venerable and Jean Mabillon against the attacks of Saint Bernard and de Rancé.

With these dangers in mind we have now to consider—if it is at all possible to consider—the most intimate characteristics of Benedictine life. Clearly no institute within the Church can claim that its way of life conduces more to the exercise and growth of virtue than another, or that it should attract a more spiritually developed character. Nor can we say, except perhaps in the broadest outline, that a particular order attracts or nourishes a particular type or temperament. There is, humanly speaking, a great deal of chance in the matter, and the natural accidents of birth and environment have their influence upon a choice of life. The boy who enters a Benedictine novitiate after passing through a Benedictine school would, for all we can see, have passed into the Jesuit novitiate, had his parents' choice fallen upon a Jesuit school; and it does not seem that we are called upon to suppose that God's providence guides to a Benedictine school those who have an *anima naturaliter Benedictina*. Others come because they have been familiar with Benedictines from their youth, as they might have been familiar with Dominicans or Carmelites. But there are certain positive qualities or potentialities that every Benedictine novice should have, and there are undoubtedly

66

certain attitudes of mind, almost mental climates, which exist in Benedictine houses.

Perhaps in the first place there is a kind of spiritual tolerance and ease, a spiritual elasticity and receptivity. The monk in normal circumstances is never alone, a pioneer, a forlorn hope, an apostle. He is one of a family, and of a family that has long and unbroken traditions; he has to learn that things cannot always be done in the best way, that the sorry scheme of things cannot be shattered to bits and then rebuilt, that he is surrounded by a large number of men who, like himself, have their own ideas and limitations, that the best intentions may be opposed and the worst condoned when the greater good of the greater number requires it. As a member of a family he comes to realize that charity is often better than zeal and sacrifice; that it is ill quarrelling in a small boat on a long voyage; that he must take from others what they have, and not demand from them what they lack; that many things are healed by time. As a superior, he may have realized that here, too, he cannot escape from the limitations of his medium; that it is in and with and for his family that he must work; that neither hand nor head could exist without the body; that he is indeed the head or the hand of this definite body and cannot leave it behind or tear it in pieces or transmute it into something rich and strange.

These considerations may seem obvious enough and equally applicable to all religious communities and, indeed, to every gathering of human beings. In a measure they are, but not in the same measure. A

THE BENEDICTINES

few religious bodies are more eremitical than Benedictines; the vast majority are less domestic in genius,
and, as has been well pointed out, are encouraged
to regard themselves as a spiritual family with some
points of resemblance to a natural one rather than
as a natural family made supernatural. The Benedictine by his profession is the member of a single
definite family, not of this family to-day and of that
to-morrow. We have said that a certain spiritual
ease is typical of Benedictine life. It is possible to
conceive a religious superior (and his subjects) as
holding that their supreme aim is to spend and be
spent for the purposes of their institute as a general
uses his soldiers, leaving the issue to God; or again
it is possible to conceive a religious superior not so
much in the figure of a wise father as of the stroke
of a boat, imposing upon others and exacting from
them his own (admittedly the best) rhythm. Neither
of these conceptions is Saint Benedict's. There should
be, ordinarily speaking, no active work on which
monks, as a body, can be called upon to spend themselves, nor was it the Founder's idea that the life
within the walls should be such as to take a direct
toll from all except the most robust. Naturally, if
the fortunes of the house are at a low ebb, almost
everything must be sacrificed to active work; if the
Church is persecuted monks (like all others) must
keep the gospel alive at all costs; but a large religious
house in normal times should not be working fever-
ishly, *enfants perdus*. In fact, we can go further
and say that the monk who in ordinary circumstances
takes to any work with a zeal which absorbs all

68

his time and energies and which burns out his fire of strength and health, is departing from what is for him the way of salvation. It is not a virtue for the monk, as it might be for the missionary, to lack time in which to attend the office, read a certain amount and mix with his community. And hence there should be in the Benedictine monk a certain restfulness, a contentment, not in doing nothing but in doing the familiar, even the monotonous and the ritual; an ability to remain physically unmoved and unexcited, to produce, in fact, that stability which his Founder made a distinguishing and on occasion a unique religious vow.

And here, too, just as Saint Benedict wrote his Rule for the ordinary man, so the Benedictine climate does not attract or develop a particular type of sanctity that is very real and of the greatest value to the Church—those sons of thunder, unconventional, even farouche, a John of the Cross, a Charles de Foucauld, a William Doyle, admirable if inimitable, who so rivet the attention and fire the imagination of men, and are sometimes taken by those outside the Church to be the most pure quintessence of sanctity.

Such men as these are led not merely by high, but by special ways. *Gratia sequitur naturam*—and in their case we may think that their nature was original and abnormal. For them the *aurea mediocritas* of the Benedictine life in community would be impossible. For the monk must not be intolerant or intransigent; he must be teachable and adaptable; and for him sanctity and the art of living on terms with many others are two aspects of the one task. Patience,

69

THE BENEDICTINES

in the widest sense of the word, must always be a
monastic virtue. A monk cannot throw himself utterly
into anything. The lines of his life, the interruptions
of the day and the loss of energy caused by the office
and spiritual duties must always keep him in check.
It is part of his obedience and of his poverty that
he cannot call his life or his time his own.

VI

THE BENEDICTINE SPIRITUAL
LIFE

1. *The Monastic Discipline.*

But we must rise a little from considering the monk
as he is to consider the supernatural aims which should
mould him. In what does the essence of the Benedictine self-discipline, the monastic ascesis lie? [*Qotd*]

For all Christians their ascesis, their effort towards
perfection, consists in making themselves at one with [*ascesis*]
the will of God, in putting off the old man and putting [*- effort*]
on Christ, in losing their soul to find it, in making of [*towards*]
God, and not of a self separate from God, the agent [*perfection*]
and centre of all energy. But there are many kinds of
souls and minds and bodies; star differeth from star;
the Father's house has many mansions, and it is
possible to achieve the common end by different
means, or to see the same means—for human intelligence is very finite—under different aspects. What,
then, is the Benedictine scheme of the spiritual life?

Growth in holiness, all will agree, consists in sub-
mitting our will to God's, in killing or mortifying
our own will as distinct from God's. This process
may be conceived as taking place in several ways;
and if, in practice, they are rarely found entirely

71

separate, yet the preponderance of one over the others marks a real difference between the various religious institutes of the Church. In all the agent of the change must be God's Holy Spirit, but we can see more easily the different workings of the human agencies.

First, then, we may imagine a soul as isolating itself from all contagion, as in a vacuum, or as if protected by every antiseptic, and we may strip from it successive layers of evil till nothing is left but what is good. This is the way of Saint John of the Cross, at least as he is generally understood; it is the way of de Rancé and, indeed, of all purely contemplative or penitential orders; it has been called a subjective way, though essentially no way can be more subjective than another.

Or, again, the whole person—body, mind and spirit—may be subjected to a careful and methodical system of training and pruning and cultivation till the wild has become the tamed, even the formal. In this way the whole of man's spiritual and intellectual life is considered as one, and the scheme under which all his activities are brought is one consistent whole, a synthesis, a culture. Here, again, something of this sort must enter into any Christian training which is both intellectual and moral; but such a way of proceeding was brought to perfection by two or three of the greatest orders of the Church during the later Middle Ages and the Reformation epoch.

Or, again, we may turn away from the individual soul with its faculties and its recesses, and away from any scheme of the Christian world, and take the good, the very good, Christian life as it may be lived here below, try to live it, and trust that by living it we shall become within what our outward conduct suggests. This last is the ascesis of Saint Benedict. His Rule lays down the framework of the religious life—prayer and work, all regulated for the individual by obedience. These, he says, are the tools of the religious life, and he might add, with the Church when she ordains a priest, *imitare quod tractas;* do you yourself resemble the pure things you touch. Novice and elder alike are bound by this framework, but with the difference that to the novice it is a rule set from without, constraining him, something almost hostile, certainly hard, while to the perfect the external rule and even the external command are part of himself and as his own will. The Rule and all its observances are consecrated, and the monk, by fulfilling with what willingness he can, gains, by his obedience, the grace of advancement. To use again the pregnant phrase of the liturgy, *percipiendo requirit, et quaerendo sine fine percipit.* It is impossible that a monk who follows the regular life of Saint Benedict's Rule as best he can should not get nearer to God. One step will lead to the next, and he will pass unperceived of himself, from darkness to light, till, as the Prologue of the Rule says, his heart is opened and he runs in the path of the commandments of God with a love unspeakably delightful. The Benedictine ascesis, therefore, does not aim at an initial material renunciation, nor at the imposition of a consistent universal

73

culture on the mind and soul. Its aim is rather
by a sober use, by friction and assimilation, to
establish a kind of equilibrium in which active or
intellectual works and interests are themselves a
spiritual discipline and become spiritualized, along
with all the powers and affections of the soul. The
Benedictine would, in part, agree with some modern
religious thinkers who urge what they have called a
double polarity in the religious life—of other-worldli-
ness and detachment, and of this-worldliness and at-
tachment.[1]   At least the Benedictine's outlook has
always been objective, taking things as they are, and
not forcing them into categories or looking upon them
as elements in a pre-arranged scheme, and it is this
that gives him his independence—good sometimes,
sometimes bad.   There should be always something
spontaneous about him, something potential, ready to
respond to what he meets.   It is this that has led
strangers to regard him as something unprofessional
among the clergy, or at least certainly not to be
classed among the ecclesiastical *gens de métier*. They
may even at times have felt, mistakenly, that even
his beliefs were held with a difference. They have
surely felt, at times, that in the ordinary affairs
and affections of life he is a humanist—*nihil hu-
manum a se alienum putat*—along with Saint Bede
the Venerable and Saint Peter the Venerable and
Mabillon, and with that great doctor of the Church,
so Benedictine in spirit, Saint Francis of Sales.

---

[1] cf. Baron von Hugel, *Eternal Life*, p. 198.

THE BENEDICTINE SPIRITUAL LIFE

2. *Benedictine Prayer.*

The question has often been asked and answered:
Are Benedictine monks contemplatives?

The word contemplative is unfortunately ambiguous. Contemplation is, in one of its meanings, a
technical religious term for a high, and, in a sense,
extraordinary (though not miraculous) degree of
prayer, in which the soul attains to God without
using any intellectual representations, and in which
the soul is conscious of God's action upon and in
her. This prayer is a free gift of God, which is
not necessarily given when a certain degree of sanctifying grace or love of God is reached, and which no
efforts, even when assisted by ordinary grace and
the infused virtues, can of themselves attain. Indeed,
it is the common opinion that while the "threshold"
(to borrow a psychological term) of contemplation is
crossed by some souls at an early stage of spiritual
growth, others, who have advanced even to sanctity
never cross it in this life.

Clearly, if a contemplative be taken to mean one who
has attained to this degree of prayer, or one belonging to an institute that aims directly at it or counts
upon attaining to it sooner or later in this life, not
even the most rigorously secluded orders—Carthusians
or Carmelite nuns—could be called contemplative,
for it would seem the case that even in such communities the number of those who reach (or who
are rewarded by) such prayer is small in proportion
to the whole body.

On the other hand, there is a degree of prayer

75

which in God's ordinary providence can be reached and should be aimed at by any soul striving after perfection. It is a prayer which resembles contemplation, in that no distinct representation or act of the will is made, but in which the supernatural element is not directly perceived or experienced. This has frequently been called active contemplation, and it is clearly not restricted to any religious order, but is attainable by religious, priests, and laymen alike; though precisely because it is attainable by those who are not religious, it should *a fortiori* come within the scope of a religious life.

But the common restriction of the term contemplative to a few rigidly enclosed orders of men and women corresponds to spiritual facts. Speaking in general, a certain form of life almost always precedes and accompanies the gift of infused contemplation, or perhaps it would be more correct to say that the Holy Spirit leads those who are destined for this gift by certain paths of life—great abstraction of life, long hours of prayer and sharp bodily austerities, with the possibility of augmenting these almost without limit. These conditions are found in certain orders—Carthusians, Trappists, Poor Clares, Carmelites—and consequently they may rightly be called contemplative orders, though the actual reason for their acquiring the name was because they did not propose as their object any active work for religion.

Whether these special conditions were verified in Saint Benedict's own monastery cannot, of course, be decided with any certainty. Most of those who

76

have meditated on the Rule would probably be disposed to think that it does not describe a life which was for its age so abstracted and austere as are the Carthusian and Trappist lives to-day. Perhaps Saint Benedict's own feeling that while many (like himself) who were called to the highest degree of prayer would receive all needful preparation in the monastery of the Rule, yet others would need something more austere, may account for the rather baffling references to a passing from the community to the eremitical life, and to the Rule as a document for beginners. In any case, we must suppose that he assumed that the overwhelming majority of his monks would live and die under the Rule, and attain under it, or at least be able to attain, to that high degree of humility and love to which he called them. There is, then, no doubt that Saint Benedict intended his monks to aspire to that degree in the spiritual life which corresponds to an advanced degree of "active" contemplation. For this, too, certain conditions of life are necessary. A certain amount of abstraction is needed, a certain austerity and quietness of life, a considerable time given each day to mental prayer and spiritual reading. These conditions, though present in individual cases for the secular priest and many of the more modern religious institutions given to active works, are not part of the framework of their daily life. The individual must create opportunities for himself, or by means of extraordinary works of virtue supply for them in other ways. But their presence is surely guaranteed by the Rule; no one who has any knowledge of the common

77

THE BENEDICTINES

Catholic teaching on prayer can read Saint Benedict's words, however carelessly, without receiving the impression that his monks were intended to be contemplatives, and in this sense, if they would be faithful to their Founder's idea on what is surely an essential point, Benedictine monks even in the twentieth century must be contemplatives. They are by their profession pledged to be men of prayer in a way that not all called to the priesthood are bound; they are bound by their profession to spend more time in the direct adoration of God than are secular priests and many religious; they can no more escape from that obligation than they can escape from obedience; it is this that makes theirs a separate vocation in the Church, and whatever works they may do, they must do in addition to, not instead of, their primary duty of prolonged prayer, vocal and mental.

Undoubtedly the majority of Benedictines throughout the world, considered either as individuals or as communities, still maintain by their lives the secular monastic tradition. Contemplative prayer, in the sense explained above, was clearly the end proposed by the leaders of the monastic revival in the first half of the nineteenth century, by the founders of the congregation of Primitive Observance, of Solesmes and of Beuron. The revived old English congregation in the early seventeenth century began its life with a magnificent tradition of contemplation and martyrdom, and the present constitutions lay down explicitly that the monks shall be true contemplatives. It may be that in some houses here and there in almost every country commitments have been inherited from other days, or the natural development of good work has gone on till it absorbs more than its due place in the life of a particular house, but in general we may perhaps say that in every monastery where the Office and its adjuncts are carried out with solemnity and are the common work of the whole community, nothing can be seriously wrong, for the sacrifice of working hours needed for this is an assertion for house and individual of the paramount claims of the supernatural and the contemplative.

3. *The Appeal to Tradition.*

The great danger in Benedictine history, as indeed in all religious history and in all things human, has been relaxation of discipline, of observance, of aspirations, of ideals. Individual monasteries and congregations, and the whole institute have now grown, now declined in fervour. Relaxation has sometimes been spoken of as a peculiarly Benedictine danger, perhaps because of Saint Benedict's studied moderation and the long Benedictine tradition of a life in dignified surroundings, which for many centuries at least and in the majority of countries has drawn its recruits from among the educated classes and those in tolerably easy circumstances, or at least by its own training has assimilated them to those classes. But in fact relaxation is the bane of all high endeavour, the phantom that comes before the ruin in all things religious.

Against relaxation, wherever found, there are many

spiritual safeguards. But it is instructive to consider what is the safeguard peculiarly Benedictine. Most other religious orders have a rigid code of legislation binding the whole body and administered by a central control under the direction of a superior with universal jurisdiction. Again and again in Benedictine history—at Cluny, at Citeaux, in St. Justina at Padua—this expedient has been tried, but in the past such centralized bodies have always either declined in their turn or separated from the Black Monks.

If no centralization is attempted, there is the Rule; but here there is the difficulty of interpretation. We can regard the Rule as binding all monks both in its positive precepts and in its omissions, as exactly as does a code of canon law; or we may regard it as we may regard the Sermon on the Mount, as a body of teaching by which to be inspired and which we may follow, each in his own way.

The second tendency has gained a certain amount of ground in recent times, perhaps rather implicitly than explicitly. Logically pressed home, it would deny that any traditional practices or works or forms of government were necessary for Benedictine monks; there would, in effect, be a Benedictine soul, but no Benedictine body. The first tendency has re-appeared whenever reform has been in the air. A written Rule that can be reasserted and kept is a light in the dark to those adrift on the tumbling seas of religious controversy; it is something fixed and visible and material. *Hoc fac ut vivas.* Both Saint Bernard and the Abbot of la Trappe attributed to the Rule an almost magical power, giving to it, in fact, as Mabillon acutely recognized, an almost metaphysical importance.

The normal Benedictine way was nobly presented by Mabillon himself. It is the enlightened guidance of the Abbot, following the best traditions of those who have gone before, and learned in all Benedictine history of the past. This is that body of "new things and old" that the Abbot is to teach to his monks; this is the divine law that he must know; and in this way every Benedictine house where there is good-will has in its midst a force that may keep it or restore it at all times.

And therefore Benedictines, perhaps more than any other religious, must know and praise men of renown, and their fathers in their generations. They will not find them speaking at variance. They themselves must know well, and think deeply upon, their Rule, and endeavour to draw from it (what it indeed contains) the very heart of their Founder's wisdom. They must go back beyond Saint Benedict, where he sends them, to Saint Basil and Cassian and the Egyptian monks. They must follow the Rule through the ages, with Paul Warnfrid and Calmet and Delatte.

Again and again in the passage of centuries a saint or doctor will stand out with the unmistakable family likeness—Saint Gregory the Great, from whom Benedictines may always learn their primary duty of prayer and how it should be related to whatever work they may be called to do for souls; Saint Bede the Venerable "in his person and his writings, as truly the pattern of a Benedictine as is Saint Thomas of a

Dominican," [1] the first great Benedictine scholar; Saint Peter the Venerable, who could at once reform and defend; Louis of Blois, who perhaps more than any other religious writer is typically Benedictine in doctrine and spirit; the saintly and humble Mabillon, the greatest of the Maurists; and, among those of our own race in the modern world, the mystic Father Augustine Baker, at first sight so angular and narrow, but in reality free and full of warmth; and the two great prelates so alike in personal holiness and intellectual power, Archbishop Ullathorne and Bishop Hedley.

And they must follow monachism wherever it goes or has gone, through all its phases and developments, mark where it failed and why, mark where it shone and endeavour to follow it there; compare the living thing with the Rule, but never force the new wine into an old bottle. They must be willing to take what is best from others and make it their own—for the greatest Benedictines have always known the customs of many lands—but they must make it their own as we try to make another's virtues our own, not by wishing or imagining ourselves to be other individualities with other powers than those we know so well in limitation and failure, but in making with what we are and what we have something as admirable—because as much part of God's design—as anything we can see abroad. They must realize that they perhaps more than any other body within the Church, have a twofold perfection (or a perfection

---

[1] Newman.

of two aspects) to strive for, the theoretical and the practical, the material and the formal, and that though the former, the material and practical, the individual's growth in virtue in whatever circumstances he is placed, is the more immediately vital, the other, the theoretical perfection of their life in all its bearings, can have the greater consequences for themselves and others. Obedience to the immediate command will always be their safety for the moment, but will not carry them always. The ultimate responsibility lies with the Abbot, but their obedience must be that of rational beings who can know the truth when they see it. They must be prepared, not to criticize, but to create.

And so it was not a mere chance that our first vision of monasticism was an England covered with great houses, with names of fable. It was the superficial covering that held the deeper truth, that it is in the individual great abbey that the flame of Benedictine life can be best and most completely seen, and that the present must always learn from and be inspired by the vision of the past.

4. *The Abbey and the Monk.*

We have passed in this brief essay, so far as seemed possible, from a view of Benedictine monachism from without, seen in the ages, to a view seen from within and at the present day. It may not be out of place in the conclusion to go outside once more, and look for a moment at the Benedictine monk and monastery as they exist all over the world.

83

THE BENEDICTINES

The normal abbey, at least after a life of some generations, will be a notable object in the district, surrounded by its own grounds and farm land. In this the most modern abbeys, in Kansas or Pennsylvania, are at one with the German and English houses of every age, and with Monte Cassino. Whatever buildings the external work of the monks may demand, the centre, architecturally as well as for purposes of administration, will be the monastery proper, normally grouped round one or more cloister-garths or courts. On one side of the main cloister (normally the north) stands the abbey church, never a mere chapel or parish church, but with something of the cathedral in its architecture, and the point to which all the lines of plan and elevation lead.

In the church the divine office will be celebrated at the fixed hours throughout the day, year in, year out. Some parts of it, and the daily conventual Mass, will be sung, and all its accompaniment of ceremonies and apparel will mark it with a solemnity and richness not found elsewhere. A Benedictine abbey should be a home of the liturgy in a special way, where many will come who in the ordinary run of their life can only hope to see the bare essentials of Christian worship. This stream of praise, always flowing and comparable (as Saint Benedict reminds us) with the everlasting chorus of dominations and powers, is in itself exceedingly impressive. In the oldest abbeys of Europe the same round of hours, with the same psalms and versicles and hymns that we now sing, was being sung to the same melodies when the yews were young that made the bows for

THE BENEDICTINE SPIRITUAL LIFE

Agincourt, when the Armada was sighting the English coasts, when Napoleon was sending forward the Guard at Waterloo, when the battle of the Marne was hanging doubtful. In the Benedictine round of prayer nothing essential is new; the psalms must be the food of the twentieth century as they were of the Egyptian solitary and the first Christians of Corinth; the hymns and prayers may have been sung in Saint Ambrose's cathedral at Milan; they were both familiar to our forbears in Glastonbury and Westminster.

Besides the church, all the monastic buildings will have a dignity, a presence. The cloisters, the refectory, the library—all these may be simple, but they will not be sordid nor severe nor confined. It is no part of Benedictine tradition that they should be. But none of the other buildings should have the richness of the church. They should not be so bare as the Cistercian houses or the Trappist, but they should not, on the other hand, have the magnificence of the Charterhouse of Pavia.

And the individual monk—how can he be described, ideal and yet not impossible? Saint Benedict says of his novice-master in the Rule that he should have a care to see if the novice seeks God in very truth, if he is devoted to the Office, to obedience, to unpleasant things; and from the body of the Rule we cannot help gathering that these three virtues—devotion, obedience and humility—are the aspects under which Saint Benedict most readily saw the whole complex of monastic duties. The monk must, then, have devotion, and that not merely as all religious and priests must have it, but called out by and focused upon the Divine Office, and that not merely as a form of prayer to be read in the breviary, but as a common exercise of the monastic family. The newcomer who regarded the Office merely as a stage on the way to a purer, more solitary prayer, alike with him who found his consolation in extra-liturgical prayer, or who looked for the time when he should be preaching instead of singing in choir, would clearly not fulfil Saint Benedict's wish.

But besides this he must have certain tendencies, part natural, part supernatural. He must be by disposition sociable—neither domineering nor individualistic nor revolutionary. He must be naturally stable, that is, willing to spend his whole life in one place, in the midst of a single society, in one work in which he will perhaps see no great change during the half-century of his monastic life. He must be ready to live in common all his life, with common meals and a host of small permissions to be got. An easy life? Perhaps if lives be compared and calculated by stress and strain and privation and penury, it would not be considered a hard life. Perhaps if full advantage were taken of every loophole and opportunity, it might be called a physically even life. But it may be found hard enough for those who are not called to it by God, and it can be made noble enough by those to whom God gives grace. For, above all, if the monk's spiritual welfare and the spiritual level of his monastery are not to suffer, he must be a man of prayer. He must be willing to

THE BENEDICTINE SPIRITUAL LIFE

spend some hours of each day [1] in the direct service
of God which does not immediately benefit the souls
of others and which curtails his active work to a
considerable degree. He must realize that as a monk
he owes this praise to God as his day's piece-work,
his *servitutis pensum;* that, apart from exceptional
circumstances, it is not a question whether missionary
or teacher or student serves God better than he does;
this prayer, liturgical or contemplative, is what God
wants of him as a Benedictine monk, the peculiar
talent that is his, the especial jewel which Benedictines
pay into the treasury of the Church.

And because prayer is the primary duty of monks,
the Benedictine and his critics have here a test which,
if applied over a considerable space of time and in
ordinary circumstances, is both desirable and infallible.
The monk who is constant in his attendance in choir,
or absent only from obedience, and faithful in his
practice of prayer, may feel that he can look to God
for all the help that is never failing to those who
are filling the particular place that God's disposition
wills for them. He can feel that his life will in
time sanctify him. This, surely, is his peace, the
Pax of his motto, the security in feeling that he
need not be perpetually searching out for himself
some better way, the peace that comes from knowing
the will of God. This, and not some imagined gar-

---

[1] The Office, including Conventual Mass, takes some three
and a half hours on the ordinary weekday; add to this at least
half-an-hour's private prayer, half-an-hour's spiritual reading
and the priest's private Mass—over five hours direct service of
God.

den of rest, some quiet, windless backwater of life, is that *secura quies, et nescia fallere vita* which has come so readily to the mind as the aptest description of monasticism. And these are for him the beginnings of life—a consciousness, ever growing more spiritual, that the soul is in God's power and sight; obedience to the will of God made tangible and clear; the regular life, whose ordinances both suppose and create holiness.

5. *Conclusion.*

What, then, is the peculiar value of the Benedictine life as an objective, visible thing in the Church and in the world to-day? All religious orders, we realize, are most valuable, not for what they do, but for what they are, in the widest, most spiritual sense. Thus the strictly contemplative orders have an influence far beyond the small circle with whom they come into direct contact. They are in a real sense witnesses, martyrs to the truth of Christianity and to the possibilities of human nature assisted by grace. The mere fact of their existence is an inspiration to weaker souls in moments of despair or doubt or lassitude. All religious, all priests, and all dedicated to any high religious ideal share in this influence in their measure; but it is not with this that we are concerned here, but rather with the particular aspects—moral and intellectual—of the full Christian life that are emphasized by Benedictines in the form of the life they lead.

Here, surely, it is the balance, the objectivity of

THE BENEDICTINE SPIRITUAL LIFE

their life that has the greatest value. Individualism,
the subjective, the analytic, the self-conscious, the
sub-conscious, the desire for self-expression and self-
realization—all the tendencies implied by these words,
which are themselves new-minted coinage—are rife
among us to-day nowhere more than in the world of
religion. They represent (who will deny?) cravings
and discoveries that the Church must take cognizance
of and satisfy when their claims are shown to be
legitimate, but they are not the whole of life.

Similarly, it is a commonplace that we live in
a world of ceaseless activity and flux and novelty, and
it cannot be but that this has its counterpart in the
life of the spirit, and produces in the heart and mind
a restlessness, a desire to be moving and changing, a
feeling that with all the changing world we are on
the brink of discovering some new way of salvation,
and that the old must go.

In contrast to this, Benedictine monachism presents
an objective form of life, sane, strong, unchanging
from year to year, a life of work and liturgical prayer
which can be seen and heard, lived in conditions
which aim at representing all that is best in the basic
family life of Christianity, aided by all human cour-
tesies, reverences and affections. It is nothing secret
or esoteric, nor an impossibility, but an ordered form
of ordinary life. It is a religious life which is free
from all that is doctrinaire or experimental. It is the
Christian life writ large for all to see, with all the
non-Christian elements removed that are normally in-
terwoven with the devout life as lived in the world.
The message of Saint Benedict is simple and direct.

THE BENEDICTINES

Work, obey, keep silent, praise God in common, and if you wish to pray to Him alone, enter the church and pray.

It is for Benedictines to see to it that they are a living commentary on the Rule, remembering that just as they hope to save their own souls by living the regular life, so by their example they may, in what small measure soever it may be, have something of the same influence over their contemporaries of to-day that their predecessors had over a chaotic and pagan Europe.